HORRIBLE SCIENCE

KU-516-351

ANGRY ANIMALS

NICK ARNOLD

Illustrated by
Tony De Saulles

Hippo

Scholastic Children's Books,
Euston House, 24 Eversholt Street,
London NW1 1DB, UK
A division of Scholastic Ltd
London ~ New York ~ Toronto ~ Sydney ~ Auckland
Mexico City ~ New Delhi ~ Hong Kong

First published in the UK by Scholastic Ltd, 2005

Text copyright © Nick Arnold, 2005
Illustrations copyright © Tony De Saulles, 2005

10 digit ISBN 0 439 96364 8
13 digit ISBN 978 0439 96364 0

Printed in the UK by CPI Bookmarque, Croydon, CR0 4TD

10 9

The right of Nick Arnold and Tony De Saulles to be identified as the
author illustrator of this work has been asserted by her in accordance with
the Copyright, Designs and Patents Act, 1988.

Papers used by Scholastic Children's Books are made from wood
grown in sustainable forests

Contents

Nick Arnold has been writing stories and books since he was a youngster, but never dreamt he'd find fame writing about angry animals. His research involved howling with wolves and dining with komodo dragons and he enjoyed every minute of it.

When he's not delving into Horrible Science, he spends his spare time eating pizza, riding his bike and thinking up corny jokes (though not all at the same time).

Tony De Saulles picked up his crayons when he was still in nappies and has been doodling ever since. He takes Horrible Science very seriously and even agreed to make a sketch inside a crocodile. Fortunately, he has made a full recovery.

When he's not out with his sketchpad, Tony likes to write poetry and play squash, though he hasn't written any poetry about squash yet.

INTRODUCTION

Nearly everyone likes animals but animals don't always like us. And this book is alive with animals that definitely don't like humans. Big dangerous beasts that kill lots of people. Angry animals and cruel creatures.

In this blood-curdling book, we'll be looking at how they kill us, why they kill us and how we fight back. So get ready for a few hairy moments. Here are some of the creatures we'll be meeting – don't they look angry? I bet they wouldn't think twice about biting your arm off. Fancy a closer look?

Well, you won't catch *me* going near them – so I've made up a character tough enough to tackle a touchy tiger with a touch of tummy-rumbles. Please put your hands together for top TV naturalist Will D Beest and his clever pet monkey, Mickey.

Will is going to help us find the world's cruellest creature and present it with this lovely trophy…

So enjoy the rest of this book! You're sure to shudder at the bloody bits but you'll also get a shocking new view of nature and maybe a new view of people too! So are you brave enough to read on? OH DON'T BE A CHICKEN! GO ON – I DARE YOU!

THE BEASTLY BASICS

Ready to find the cruellest creature? Er, hold on a minute – I've just thought of something. This creature could be any one of up to FIFTY MILLION types of animal (scientists call them species) on Earth. And how on Earth do we sort through them all?

Sorry, readers, but before we can start looking, we'll need to organize the animals. Here are a few simple questions to help us…

1 What major group of animals does the species belong to?
2 What does it eat?
3 Where does it live?

And here are one or two useful science words…
Vertebrate = ver-tee-brate = animal with a backbone
Invertebrate = in-ver-tee-brate = animal without a backbone. They're a bit spineless - ha ha.

The Horrible Science animal group guide
Presented by Mickey the Monkey and various animals…

I'm a vertebrate and so are you.

We crabs are invertebrates and so are microbes, worms, insects, scorpions and jellyfish.

The main groups of vertebrates are fish, amphibians, reptiles, birds and mammals.

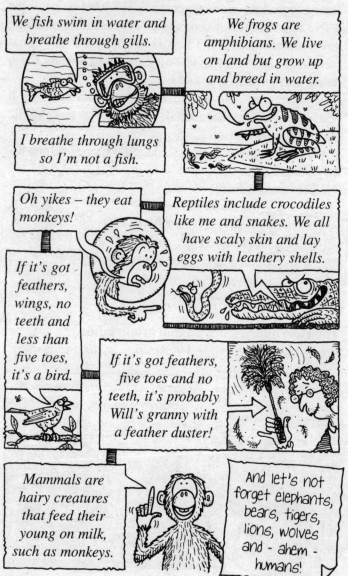

We fish swim in water and breathe through gills.

We frogs are amphibians. We live on land but grow up and breed in water.

I breathe through lungs so I'm not a fish.

Oh yikes – they eat monkeys!

Reptiles include crocodiles like me and snakes. We all have scaly skin and lay eggs with leathery shells.

If it's got feathers, wings, no teeth and less than five toes, it's a bird.

If it's got feathers, five toes and no teeth, it's probably Will's granny with a feather duster!

Mammals are hairy creatures that feed their young on milk, such as monkeys.

And let's not forget elephants, bears, tigers, lions, wolves and - ahem - humans!

Well, that monkey's certainly got brains! Now I hope you haven't got a sicky stomach because the next bit's about how to sort out animals according to what they eat. And it's going to be terribly tasteless even if the facts are easy to digest...

Disgusting dinner-time details

Like you, every species of animal has a favourite food...

• Meat-eaters eat meat (hey who said science was hard!). The posh name for them is *carnivores* and the animals they eat are called their prey. Your pet cat and dog are carnivores and so are tigers. (Mind you, a tiger would happily chomp on your cat and dine on your dog so you'd best keep them apart.)

• Meat-eaters that eat dead animals are called *scavengers*. They like food with a bit of body. Many carnivores eat any dead animals they find – even if they're manky and maggoty. Full-time scavengers include vultures.

• Plant-eaters eat plants. (I bet you bought this book to find that out!) Brainy biology boffins call them *herbivores* and examples include elephants and hippos.

9

- Animals that eat plants and animals are called *omnivores*. (By the way, I expect you're an omnivore – otherwise known as a steak and salad scoffer.)

- Creatures that eat insects are *insectivores*. I bet they love their grub(s). Examples include aardvarks (they're a species of African mammal, just in case you're wondering).

Foul feeding-time quiz

OH NO! Will's attempt to feed the animals at the Anytown Zoo has turned into a disaster! All the animals have been given the wrong food! Can you match the food to the animal that eats it?

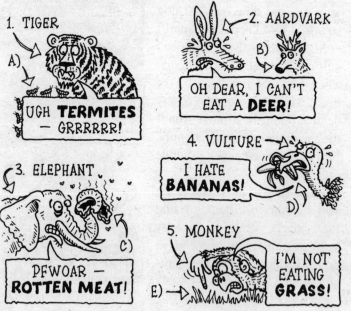

10

Meat-eaters scoff plant-eaters, plant-eaters scoff plants and so on. Scientists show these feeding choices in special diagrams called food chains or food webs (this is nothing to do with spiders' webs or webbed feet). Confused? Here's some fantastic food facts to feed your brain…

Angry animals fact file

NAME: Food webs and chains

THE BASIC FACTS: 1 Every animal eats plants or other animals or both.

2 Here's a food web for a wolf: ➤ = EATS

WOLF — HMMM DELICIOUS!

OOER!

EEEEK!

MOUSE — HARE — ELK

GULP!

BERRIES — GRASS — LEAVES

11

3 A single set of links in a food web is called a food chain, but it's nothing to do with bicycle chains or the things that ghosts rattle.

THE ANGRY DETAILS: Food chains mean animals depend on one another...
• If the plant-eaters die, the meat-eaters die too because they've got nothing to eat.
• If the meat-eaters die, the plant-eaters increase their numbers and guzzle all the plants. Then they die because they've got nothing to eat. So I guess meat-eaters are doing them a favour by eating them!

YEAH, THANKS A LOT!

Horrible animal homes

And finally, here's how to sort animals according to where they live… Every animal lives in a place called a habitat, and each animal is well-suited to living there. So if you want to sound breathtakingly brainy, you could say…

EVERY SPECIES IS ADAPTED TO LIFE IN ITS HABITAT.

SIMPKINS — I'M SPEECHLESS!

MR BOTTOMLY THE BIOLOGY TEACHER

Anyway, to prove this point, we've set up an evil experiment. Here are three animals in their habitats.

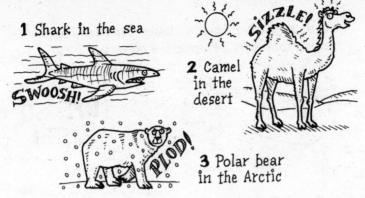

1 Shark in the sea

SWOOSH!

2 Camel in the desert

SIZZLE!

3 Polar bear in the Arctic

PLOD!

But what if we moved them around? The shark's in the Arctic, the polar bear's in the desert, and we've chucked the camel in the sea...

1 The shark's gills are adapted to breathing oxygen dissolved in the water. In the air it's gasping and now it's frozen solid. Anyone fancy shark fishfingers?

2 The polar bear's thick fur is adapted for life in the cold. It's over-heating right now.

3 The camel is adapted for life without too much water but it's sunk in the sea. Hmm – maybe we should have given it a snorkel and flippers...

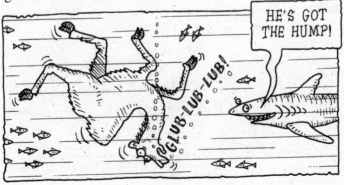

HE'S GOT THE HUMP!

GLUB-LUB-LUB!

Well, those are the beastly basics. And now let's get searching for the world's cruellest creature…

NOT SO FAST!

Oh what now, Will?

YOU HAVEN'T EXPLAINED WHY ANIMALS ATTACK US.

IT'S PROBABLY BECAUSE HUMANS ANNOY US…

OOPS – silly me! We can't go looking for animals until we know *why* they attack us. I mean, they might attack us before we know we're in danger. 'Scuse me whilst I have an attack of the n-n-n-n-n-erves…

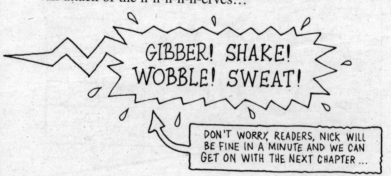

GIBBER! SHAKE! WOBBLE! SWEAT!

DON'T WORRY, READERS, NICK WILL BE FINE IN A MINUTE AND WE CAN GET ON WITH THE NEXT CHAPTER …

ANGRY ANIMAL ATTACKS

This is a *dangerous* book. In our search for the world's cruellest creature we could be attacked at any minute! We might suffer the same fate as these poor people…

South Africa, 1960

A teenage boy thought he'd been touched by a piece of seaweed. Then he saw a shark biting his leg. Desperately he gouged at the shark's eyes. But his hand slipped into the shark's mouth and its sharp teeth stripped the flesh from his fingers. Moments later the shark let him go but as the boy tried to escape, the killer fish bit his side. The terrified boy swam for his life through a cloud of his own blood…

Northern Australia, 1981

Blood spurted from the man's body as the huge crocodile tried to pull him into the deep water. Bravely, the 12-year-old girl leapt into the river and grabbed the man's arm. She gritted her teeth – she wouldn't let go even as the man screamed in pain when the croc's jaws bit deeper into his flesh…

Kenya, Africa, 1900s

The little girl sang as she ran barefoot over the dusty earth. She never saw the lion stalking her through the long grass and making ready to spring. The next thing she felt was the blow that threw her to the ground, the sharp teeth biting her leg and the ROAR that seemed to fill the whole world…

You'll be pleased to know that the boy swam to the shore, and the 12-year-old girl pulled the man from the water and drove him to safety, and the little girl was rescued from the lion. But other victims have been less fortunate. So why do people get attacked? Are we really that tasty? We asked Will D Beest…

In fact Will's given us *loads* of answers…

1 Meat-eaters (carnivores) usually kill to eat. Some meat-eaters set out to hunt humans but others only attack if they mistake us for their usual prey. Well, that's their excuse anyway. Some brave scientists have studied why tigers and lions eat us, and you can snap up their findings on page 103.

2 Herbivores aren't best pleased about being eaten, so they try to fight back. And herbivores sometimes attack us if they think we're trying to attack them.

3 Many animals attack us if they think we're trying to invade their territory (that's the area where they live and feed).

4 Animals are more likely to attack us if they're angry.

• Injured animals are sure to be more bad-tempered. This is why teachers with toothache are especially dangerous.

• Caged animals are often stressed and likely to attack anyone who ventures into their cage. That's why I wouldn't get too close to Mr Bottomly right now…

5 Male animals are extra-grumpy in the breeding season because they often have to fight with other males to win a mate. And they might take their bad temper out on us.

6 Female animals often try to protect their young if you go too close to them.

7 Male animals may try to protect their families.

8 Larger animals are always bad-tempered when they're hungry. Plant-eaters often get hungry if humans take all the best grazing land for their sheep and cattle.

To make matters worse, loads of different animals seem willing to have a go at us. In the next quiz there are five creatures that have attacked humans and two that are as harmless as a toy puppy. So which is which?

17

The hair-raising harmless and harmful quiz

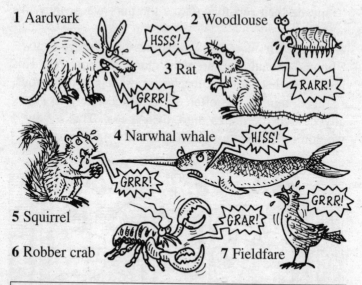

1 Aardvark

2 Woodlouse

3 Rat

4 Narwhal whale

5 Squirrel

6 Robber crab

7 Fieldfare

Answers:

1 HARMFUL In 2001 a Scottish tourist in Africa was tossed in the air by an angry aardvark. The tourist broke four ribs. It must have been real 'aard luck.

2 HARMLESS Woodlice eat rotting wood so they're only a menace to your teacher's wooden leg.

3 HARMFUL Rats attack sleeping people (this makes the humans ratty too). But according to scientists it's nothing personal. Rats eat other dead rats and they think a sleeping person is a bit on the dead side too. Mind you, that's no excuse for putting your pet rat in your sister's bed…

4 HARMLESS (as long as you don't upset it) Despite its spiky horn, the narwhal has never spiked a human. The word "narwhal" means "corpse whale" and comes from its habit of swimming belly-up.

5 HARMFUL When wacky inventor Mike Madden tested his bird-feeding hat – complete with built-in bird house and nut tray – he was attacked by a savage squirrel. Mike suffered neck injuries (this is honestly true so stop shaking your head).

6 HARMFUL And talking about nuts, in 1957, 26 sleeping people were killed on a Red Sea island by robber crabs who mistook their heads for coconuts. Now that's what I call shell-shock!

7 HARMFUL (sort of) So you think a cute little bird like a fieldfare wouldn't harm you? You're right! But when people get too close to fieldfare nests, the beastly birds bombard them with poo. Anyone fancy fighting off fifty filthy flapping fouling fieldfares?

Bet you never knew!
Talking about our feathered fiends – I mean friends – in 2004 a postman was painfully pecked by a ferociously fierce pheasant. That must have been a deeply un-pheasant experience.

A very important announcement...

I've just received a very important email from the Cruellest Creature Competition judges.

> ### The Cruellest Creature Competition Judges' Ruling
>
> We've received hundreds of entries for the Cruellest Creature Competition, but to save time we're only considering...
> - Animals with backbones.
> - Animals that kill lots of people.
>
> Hope your readers aren't too disappointed!

Well, it looks like bees, wasps, jellyfish, spiders and scorpions are out of the running because they don't have backbones. And it's goodbye to birds and loads of small creatures because they hardly ever kill people. Oh dear – these animals are angry at being left out!

Time to make our escape. Tell you what, let's dive into the next chapter!

Er, maybe not...

Savage Sharks

First up in our crazy quest for the World's Cruellest Creature is the great white shark. Now I bet you can't wait to get your teeth into some savagely shocking slaughter-in-the-water shark stories ... but because this is a respectable educational book we're going to have a few facts instead.

Don't worry – we'll check out the bloody bits on page 24!

Angry animals fact file

NAME OF CREATURE: Great white shark

TYPE OF ANIMAL: Fish

DIET: Carnivore – eats fish and mammals such as cute seals and dolphins and the odd not-so-cute human.

NUMBER OF PEOPLE KILLED*: Great white sharks kill fewer than two people per year. (On average, all types of shark only kill about 12 people a year.)

WHERE THEY LIVE: Cool oceans all around the world. For some strange reason they like to hang around islands where seals live. Any guesses why?

* All figures in this book are estimates and may vary from year to year.

SIZE: Females are larger than males and they can be up to 4.5 metres long. Some great whites grow to over 6 metres and can weigh 3 tonnes.

FEARSOME FEATURES:

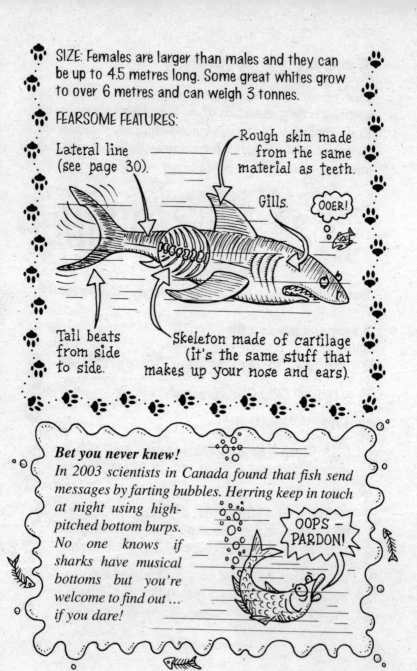

Lateral line (see page 30).

Rough skin made from the same material as teeth.

Gills.

OOER!

Tail beats from side to side.

Skeleton made of cartilage (it's the same stuff that makes up your nose and ears).

Bet you never knew!

In 2003 scientists in Canada found that fish send messages by farting bubbles. Herring keep in touch at night using high-pitched bottom burps. No one knows if sharks have musical bottoms but you're welcome to find out ... if you dare!

OOPS – PARDON!

Anyway here are some shark facts that we do know – well, some people know them…

Four facts that not a lot of people know about great white sharks

1 Great white sharks hatch from eggs whilst still inside their mums. They keep alive by eating unhatched eggs. That's right – they gobble up their unborn brothers and sisters.

2 A great white shark has a "belly button" … on its throat! It's the mark where the yolk of the egg connected to its body.

3 Once it's born, a baby great white shark has to hide from adult sharks who might try to eat it. Even the baby's mum might try to munch it. And you thought you had it tough…

4 As a great white shark grows older it gets greyer on top and bigger round the middle – just like some humans! Of course, the sharks are fairly grey on top already – the colour helps them to blend in with the dark sea when seen from above.

Ruthless relatives

So you thought your relatives were bad? Wait 'til you meet some of the other human-killers in the shark family! They're not into happy families, but they might want to play "SNAP" with you…

Name: Bull shark
Size: 2.1 to 3.5 metres long.
Lives: Warm seas close to coasts; sometimes swims up rivers.
Dreadful danger: The brutal bull shark chomps any humans it finds in the river. This antisocial habit makes it a bigger killer than the great white.

Name: Tiger shark
Size: 3 to 6 metres long.
Lives: Warm oceans just like the ones people like to swim in.
Dreadful danger: The terrible tiger shark isn't too fussy about food and will happily eat a human. This gives a totally new meaning to the phrase "feeding the fish".

Now, I suppose you're wondering what it's like to be attacked by one of these savage sharks.

Well, it's no fun at all… In 1994 South African surfing champion Andrew Carter was grabbed by a shark. He said: "I remember its power. I felt like my bones were being crushed."

Andrew screamed as the water turned red around him, but oddly enough like many shark-bite victims, he didn't feel much pain. As the shark opened its jaws to take a bigger bite, Andrew shoved his surfboard into the shark's giant gob. A lucky wave carried Andrew to shore.

He was indeed lucky. The shark attacked Andrew's friend Bruce and bit off his leg. Bruce died of his injuries.

Now for another savage shark story – this is how the paper might have reported it. In bite-sized chunks, naturally…

The Matawan News

CRACKPOT CAPTAIN'S SHARK SCARE STORY!

Captain Thomas Cottrell says he's spotted a shark in the creek just 100 metres from our town.

Capt. Cottrell

"I saw its dark grey shape in the water!" puffed the potty pensioner as he hurried into town to alert locals. But everyone laughed at the oddball old-timer.

The News says...

WHAT A FISHY TALE!

So old Captain Cottrell's seen a shark? Like heck he has! Matawan folk won't be panicked by this far-fetched fishy tale. Our town is 16 km from the sea and the creek is too shallow for sharks. So grab your towels and enjoy a dip! Yes — let's ignore that strange old sea dog!

The Matawan News

STOP THESE SHOCK SHARK SLAYINGS!

Matawan is reeling after the savage shark attacks that killed two local lads and injured another. First the fearsome fish seized young Lester Stilwell when he was swimming with friends.

At first no one knew it was a shark, and when have-a-go hero Stanley Fisher tried to rescue Lester's body the fearsome fish bit Fisher's leg off. He died later in hospital.

As terror gripped the town, men piled into boats and dropped dynamite into the creek to blast the shark to bits.

But the shark bit back. As Joseph Dunn and his friends tried to flee the water – the savage shark chomped the young lad's leg.

The News Says...
SORRY READERS!
We would like to apologize for the misprint in the News of two days ago. When we said "enjoy a dip" we actually meant to say "that shark's gonna let rip!"

The facts of this story are true, but modern experts aren't too sure what species of shark carried out the attack. Some sharks were caught near the scene but no one knew which one was the killer. Most people blamed a great white, which had bones in its stomach, but a bull shark may have been the guilty fish.

And while we're talking about being eaten by a shark you might be feeling a trifle peckish. If so, here's a revolting recipe to relish...

THE HORRIBLE SCIENCE COOK BOOK
Shark Stomach Soup

This soup is based on items that were really found in sharks' stomachs...

INGREDIENTS
A horse's head
Bits of bicycle
A human arm
One dog's backbone
One whole goat (make sure it's 100 per cent dead!)
Shark's stomach juices
Salt and pepper

WHAT YOU NEED
A big pot
A clothes peg for your nose – your soup is going to pong!

A supply of sick bags

WHAT YOU DO
1. Stir the ingredients in the big pot. Or you could pour them into a shark's stomach.
2. Heat gently until the sickening stink is so bad you can't bear it any more.
3. Serve your soup before the neighbours complain and enjoy the sight of all your friends throwing up.
4. Pour the rest of the soup down the toilet.
5. Go into hiding.

Bet you never knew!
The human arm belonged to an Australian gangster named James Smith. It turned up inside a tiger shark in 1935. One of Smith's crooked mates confessed to killing the criminal and dumping his body in a metal box. He cut off Smith's arm because it stuck out of the box...

Shock horror – here's some good news on shark attacks!

The GOOD news – your chances of being hurt by a shark are about 20 times more teeny than a termite's toenail. The number of people bitten by sharks in the USA every year is about one quarter of the number who have to go to hospital in New York after vicious hamster attacks. You've actually got ten times more chance of being killed by a falling coconut than being killed by a shark.

The BETTER news – great white sharks often attack because they mistake us for seals. They usually only bite us to find out a bit more about us (or do I mean a "bite" more about us?). Some scientists think that sharks aren't keen on our taste and that's why they often take just one bite and then swim off.

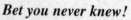

Bet you never knew!
US shark scientist David Baldridge tested how fussy sharks can be. He lowered a rat into a pool of sharks but the sharks refused the rat.

HORRIBLE HEALTH WARNING!
Lowering your pet hamster into a pool of sharks is strictly against the law!!!

So are sharks dangerous? You bet! Sharks bite first and ask questions afterwards (well, come to think of it, they don't ask questions at all). What's more, even a friendly nibble from a great white can bite you in half like a jelly baby. Anyway, despite the danger, Will D Beest wants to show us how a great white shark attacks its prey. Now is that stupid – or what?

Will D Beest in … Short shark shock

*Yes, it really is called chum. This is the usual method of attracting sharks.

DRAT! The attack was too fast to tell you what was happening. Fortunately we have the technology to show you an action replay…

1 The shark sniffs blood in the water 0.5 km away.

2 The lateral line on its side feels movement in the water 100 metres away.

3 The shark scents the dead fish.

4 When it's 25 cm away the shark senses electrical currents in the water. The shark shoots its jaws forward to grab a bigger bite and then it…

5 Bites! Each triangular tooth is rammed into the victim.

6 The shark often draws back after the first bite to allow its victim to bleed to death. Fortunately in this case, the "victim" was a rather silly rubber ring.

The savage shark survival quiz

Naturally you're far too sensible to be caught by a great white shark, aren't you? And that's why you've just been signed up for this cruel quiz…

WARNING!
IF YOU LOSE THE QUIZ YOU GET EATEN BY A SHARK!!!

You're having the holiday to end all holidays – but will it prove to be the end of YOU?

SHARK ISLAND
POPULATION ~~136~~ ~~135~~ 134

GRORK!

1 Where's the safest place to swim?
a) Next to the Shark Island Fishing Competition – I can watch it underwater.
b) Next to the seals. I'll love playing with them.
c) Close to the lifeguard's hut.

2 What's the safest thing to wear?
a) My bright yellow stripy swimming cozzie (it'll scare the sharks away) plus my lucky charm for extra good fortune.
b) A suit of armour.
c) An ordinary swimming costume.

3 What's the best anti-shark protection?
a) A bottle of shampoo.
b) My shark-blaster bomb-stick.
c) My pet dolphin.

ANTI SHARK

4 Anything else you've forgotten?

a) My surfboard – I could surf a wave and escape the shark.

b) A dead sheep to feed the shark with – that way it won't be hungry for me.

c) Nothing.

5 The shark attacks you – what's the best thing to do?

a) Reason with it in a calm but firm tone of voice.

b) Stick my finger in its eye or punch its nose.

c) Scream very loudly and wave my arms in the air.

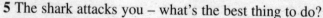

Answers:

1 c) The lifeguard could help you. Anywhere with juicy dead fish or seals is going to be a magnet for great whites.

2 c) Experts call yellow "yum-yum yellow" because the colour seems to attract sharks. They could mistake the stripes for a stripy fish. The armour is a bad choice because it causes electrical currents that sharks sense. Oh yes – and you could sink to the bottom of the sea and drown. Mind you, shark scientists do wear a kind of armour called chain-mail to protect themselves against smaller sharks.

3 a) Shampoo contains sodium lauryl sulphate – a chemical that puts sharks off when you squirt it into their mouths. I expect they "hair off" in the opposite direction. The bomb could injure a shark and make it more dangerous. In the 1950s US scientists tried to train Simo the dolphin to fight sharks, but scared Simo scarpered from larger sharks. Sounds like a sensible Simo to me.

4 c) The surfboard is seal-shaped when seen from underneath so it might draw sharks. Experiments by US scientist A. Peter Klimley show that sharks hate sheep so they won't eat it. It was a woolly-minded idea anyway…

5 b) If a shark grabs you, fighting back is your only chance.

WHAT YOUR SCORE MEANS

5 Shark survivor! You're clued up and know exactly what to do. There's NO WAY you'll end up as a shark snack!

3–4 Careful now! You made a few silly mistakes and you could be chancing your arm … or possibly your leg!

1–2 Accident waiting to happen. You've got it coming!

0 YOU'RE A DEAD LOSS! Well, dead actually.

Bet you never knew!
1 In 1957, after a series of savage shark attacks, the South African government ordered a warship to drop underwater bombs on the sharks. They probably wanted to give the animals a short shark shock – but it didn't work. The attacks continued.
2 Talking about fighting sharks … in ancient Hawaii prisoners were forced to fight hungry sharks armed only with a shark's tooth. I expect the fights took place at tooth-hurty in the afternoon (or is this just tooth horrible tooth think about?).

OOH – I'M TERRIFIED!

Well, no matter if you're a secret shark scientist or a fully fledged selachophobic (that means someone who's scared of sharks), you've got to agree that sharks must be strong contenders for the Cruellest Creature Competition – but wait, here's a late entry…

WANTED FOR CRUEL CRIMES

The Red-bellied Piranha Fish

GRRR!

Last seen: Lurking in South American rivers.

Crimes include stripping animals to their bones in a few murderous minutes, turning especially nasty if they get trapped in a drying-out lake.

Known associates: Some species of piranha fish are vegetarian. I bet they could terrify a healthy fruit salad.

BEWARE! The piranha is a fearsomely fierce fish so don't dip your toe in the river to find out what will happen. And DEFINITELY DON'T bring one home to make friends with your pet goldfish…

BUBBLES BEFORE

BUBBLES AFTER

Hmm – so you think your school's bad? I bet you'd want to be expelled from a school of piranhas even faster! But what's this? The judges don't seem to agree…

But just when you thought it was safe to go back into the
river, something else raises its ugly head...

You can turn the page now, but be careful where you put
your fingers!

CRAFTY CROCODILES

The creature in this chapter could put you off messing about on the river for life – well, your life won't last five minutes if you get too close. It's true! Just look at these crucial crocodile facts…

Angry animals fact file

NAME OF CREATURE: Nile crocodile

TYPE OF ANIMAL: Reptile

FEARSOME FEATURES:

Yes, crocs do have a heart – and it's not too different from yours!

Hard palate between mouth and nose protects croc's squishy brain from a victim's kick in the gob.

K-PLOOP!

Scaly waterproof skin

X-RAY VIEW

SHNAP!

Waterproof eggs

Flaps in nose, ears and throat keep mucky river water out. These are vital since crocs have no lips to seal their mouths.

Powerful tail can break a deer's legs.

DIET: Carnivore – eats fish, mammals, birds and anything it can scrunch. Crocs only need to feed once a week – but they can still kill a human.

NUMBER OF PEOPLE KILLED: Several hundred per year.

WHERE THEY LIVE: Rivers and lakes in Africa and Madagascar.

SIZE: Up to 4.88 metres long. The bigger crocs are the older ones but luckily they lose their teeth with age. Still, you could be "gummed" to death.

Bet you never knew!
Most reptiles don't have voices, but crocs do. Their roars sound like distant thunder – I'd hate to hear them singing in the bath first thing in morning!

Ruthless relatives

You'll be delighted to read that most other species of crocodiles and alligators never attack humans. But you'll be less delighted to learn that some of these cruel creatures happily harm humans…

Name: Alligator
Size: Males are up to 3.66 metres long.
Lives: South and Central America, southern USA, China.
Dreadful danger: American alligators are relaxed reptiles when it comes to humans. In the USA they only kill about one person a year. Mind you, that doesn't make them safe. If you bathed in their rivers they'd probably turn your bath-time into barf-time.

Name: Saltwater crocodile (known to its friends as "saltie").

Size: Up to 6 metres long.

Lives: Rivers and coasts in southern Asia and the Pacific including Australia. They've been spotted up to 970 km from land.

Dreadful danger: These angry animals reckon their stretch of the river belongs to them and trespassers will be eaten. We're talking about two people per year in Australia and many more in the rest of the world.

Spot the difference competition

Can you spot THREE differences between these pictures?

CROC

ALLIGATOR

Answers:

1 The crocodile has a more pointed snout.

2 You can see a lower tooth on each side of the croc's jaw.

3 The croc buries her eggs in a nest of sand. The alligator makes her nest from rotting plants.

Cruel crocodile childhood

And now for a tale of woe that will have you shedding tears by the bucketful (crocodile tears, naturally).

A few years ago crocodile scientists discovered that mother crocodiles have a caring sharing side. Yes, they're really kind-hearted crocs.

Having laid and buried about 60 eggs, Ma Croc patiently hangs about for three months waiting for the babies to hatch. This is vital since many creatures, including lizards, birds and monkeys, like nothing better than a crocodile-egg omelette. But Mother's there to protect her nest...

When they're ready to hatch, the cute little baby crocs call to their mum and gently, oh so gently, she digs them from the sand. With tender care she carries them to the river in her giant jaws. Ahhh isn't that sweet... I just hate to tell you that most of the those ever-so-cute baby crocs get guzzled by lizards and fish and snakes and yes, other crocs. In fact 99 per cent of them don't get to grow up. Oh dear.

Bet you never knew!

1 Alligator mums care for their young in a similar way, but they take the babies to a special pool known as a 'gator hole. And I bet the hole's a hole lot safer.

2 Alligator nests get re-used over the years, slowly growing into swampy islands. Trees grow on the islands and birds called egrets nest in the trees. Ma Alligator keeps other creatures away from the nest, so it's only fair that when a baby bird falls from the nest the reptile gets a little reward ... oh well, it's a cheep-cheep snack.

Crocs and alligators sound completely cruel and I certainly wouldn't want to be a croc dentist. But there was a zany zoologist (a scientist who studies animals) who would have loved the job. Unlike other naturalists of his time, Charles Waterton (1782–1864) didn't want to hear about animals from travellers – he wanted to study them in their natural habitats. Wacky Waterton enjoyed wrestling with a cayman (that's a relative of the crocodile). But was he quite as strange as everyone said?

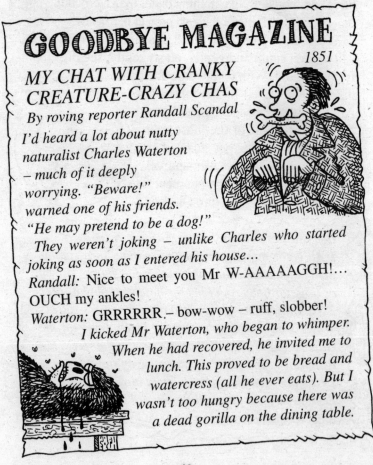

GOODBYE MAGAZINE

1851

MY CHAT WITH CRANKY CREATURE-CRAZY CHAS

By roving reporter Randall Scandal

I'd heard a lot about nutty naturalist Charles Waterton – much of it deeply worrying. "Beware!" warned one of his friends. "He may pretend to be a dog!"

They weren't joking – unlike Charles who started joking as soon as I entered his house…

Randall: Nice to meet you Mr W-AAAAAGGH!… OUCH my ankles!

Waterton: GRRRRRR.– bow-wow – ruff, slobber!

I kicked Mr Waterton, who began to whimper. When he had recovered, he invited me to lunch. This proved to be bread and watercress (all he ever eats). But I wasn't too hungry because there was a dead gorilla on the dining table.

RS: What's that dead gorilla doing on the dining table?
CW: I'm cutting it up – would you like to look at the liver?

RS (turning green): I'm not too fond of liver.

After lunch Mr Waterton took me on a tour of his house to scare me with his collection of home-made monsters, created from bits of animal bodies. This was followed by a hop along a high wall. The interview continued up a high tree.

RS: What are we doing up a tree?

CW: I come here to watch birds and wildlife on the ground. I like to talk to the birds.

After the fire brigade rescued me from the tree, the interview continued on the ground.

RS: You're famous for your travels in South America where you studied the local animals. Is it true that you tried to get a vampire bat to drink your blood?

CW: Yes, but the bats weren't biting. I had more luck with the flesh-eating bugs. I made notes on how I felt as they bored into me.

RS: You mean the bugs were boring?

CW: No – they were quite interesting, actually.

RS: So how did you catch a cayman in South America?

CW: I wanted to study a cayman close up. So in 1819 I paid some natives to catch one using a rat as bait. But the cayman wasn't best pleased at being caught and no one dared to go near it.

RS: Except you…?

CW: Catching the beast was easy – if I can just demonstrate…

At this point Mr W asked me to crouch like a crocodile. A moment later he jumped on my back and forced my arms backwards.

RS: OUCH – get off me!

CW: So you see it was quite easy… Excuse me I have an itch.

Suddenly Mr W leapt off me and began to scratch the back of his head with his big toe. After this disgraceful display, Mr W offered to show me how he caught a giant snake using the braces that held up his trousers. A few hours later, he untied me and I made my escape…

I would like to finish my report by saying that everything they say is true, and Mr W is more nutty than a squirrel's pantry! I need a holiday!

OK, so I made up Randall, but all these freaky facts about Charles Waterton are truthfully true.

Bet you never knew!

1 Charles Waterton was one of the first people ever to turn his garden into a nature reserve. In Waterton's garden, no one was allowed to harm any animal except rats.

THAT'S UNFAIR!

YES – I SMELL A RAT!

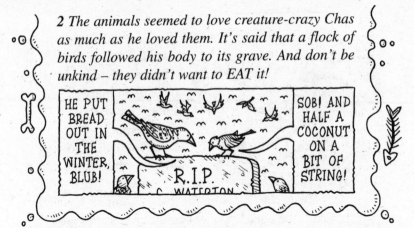

2 The animals seemed to love creature-crazy Chas as much as he loved them. It's said that a flock of birds followed his body to its grave. And don't be unkind – they didn't want to EAT it!

HE PUT BREAD OUT IN THE WINTER, BLUB!

R.I.P. C. WATERTON

SOB! AND HALF A COCONUT ON A BIT OF STRING!

I must say, I don't think it's terribly sensible to wrestle with caymans or crocodiles. And if you tried to wrestle with these celebrity crocs you might end up missing some vital body bits…

Top of the crocs

WHAH!

At number 5...

Sweetheart (Yes, that's an odd name for a huge flesh-eating reptile but read on and all will be revealed.)
Home: Sweet's Look-out Billabong, Australia. (Told you!)
Hobbies: Crunching outboard motors.

Fate: Apart from biting boats, Sweetheart never did anyone any harm but sadly the saltie (that means saltwater croc, remember?) died when scientists tried to knock him out to move him away from people.

At number **4**...

DRiBBLE!

Solomon

Home: A wildlife park in Australia.

Hobbies: Eating and basking in the sun.

Fate: One day in 1997, wildlife-park worker Karla Bradl was showing Solomon the saltie to some tourists when the cunning croc chomped her leg. Karla's dad (the park boss) jabbed the croc's eyes until it let go and luckily Solomon was old and partly toothless. In fact, Karla had just said: "If I ever get grabbed, I'd rather it be this one!"

I expect Solomon felt a bit down in the mouth. But you'll be pleased to hear that Karla's dad refused to let Solomon be killed saying "...he wouldn't bite anything with bones in it." Except his daughter of course!

At number **3**...

SKRUNCH!

Kwena

Home: Okovango Swamp, Botswana, Africa.

Hobbies: Gobbling goats (and people).

Fate: When Kwena was killed in 1968, the 5.8-metre killer croc had two goats, half a donkey and half a woman in its stomach.

We've nearly reached Number One – but first...

Bujang Senang

Home: Lupar River, Sarawak, Borneo.

Hobbies: Football and eating people. (To be honest, I'm not too sure if the croc even liked football, but the local team named itself after the revolting reptile.)

Fate: In the 1980s and 1990s this crafty croc crunched dozens of people but always managed to hide from hunters. And a witch doctor's bid to catch the croc by magic spells spelled failure.

AND NOW FOR THE BIG NUMBER 1 – AND IT REALLY IS BIG…

Gustave

Home: Burundi, Africa.

Hobbies: Scaring hippos and eating people.

Fate: Terrified locals claimed the gigantic 1-tonne croc had eaten over THREE HUNDRED people. In March 2003 an international team of scientists tried to trap the croc in a giant cage or using spring traps. But the crafty croc dodged the traps … until one day he disappeared, never to be seen again. Maybe he'd gone to a croc-and-roll concert…

I hope you're hungry for crafty croc and artful alligator attack facts because here's a cruel quiz to chew over. My mate Honest Bob has five facts – but beware! Bob's as dodgy as a second-hand dodgem car. The facts get more and more freaky. Can you spot where the facts stop being true and start being false? Over to you, Bob!

HONEST BOB'S "CAN YOU BELIEVE IT?" QUIZ

TRUE/FALSE
1. In 2001 a Florida alligator tried to eat ... a live horse!
2. In 2001 a camper in Australia woke to find himself in bed with ... a crocodile!
3. In 2002 an African crocodile was bitten by ... a man!
4. In 2004 a group of children took an alligator ... to school by bus!
5. In 2005 a teacher was attacked on the toilet by ... an alligator that lived in the sewer!
6. In 2005 scientists found a fossil crocodile ... with wings!

Answers:
1 TRUE You'll be pleased to hear that the horse survived its injury and is now in a stable condition – geddit?
2 TRUE The crafty croc had crawled into the man's sleeping bag but another camper frightened it away.
3 TRUE Mac Bosco Chawinga was grabbed by the croc but escaped after biting its snout – and that's snout too funny if you're a croc.

4 TRUE The children tied the alligator up with clothes but I bet their teachers were terrified.

5 FALSE Alligators don't live in sewers although they can be swept into them by heavy rains. If the teacher had been bitten he'd have nipped in the toilet, been nipped on the toilet and nipped out even faster!

6 FALSE No croc ever had wings. Oh don't tell me you fell for *that!!!*

All this talk of ruthless reptiles raises quite a queasy question. How exactly do crocs and alligators attack humans? Oh well, I'm sure you don't want to know – it's really *very* gruesome…

Well, I've got a uneasy feeling that Will D Beest is about to find out.

Will D Beest in … Croc crack!

Ouch, I bet that hurt, Will! When Australian wildlife ranger Charlie Finn was attacked by a saltie, the cruel croc grabbed his arm. Charlie said later: "I heard the sounds of bones crunching. It was pretty horrible." The croc went into a death roll, but luckily it let go of Charlie's chewed arm.

Still, this is all scientifically fascinating, and whilst Will's recovering in hospital, we've asked the croc that did the damage to tell us about his eating habits…

Crunch-time for crocs

We crocodiles drown our prey – including humans. That way they don't fight back and we can guzzle them at leisure.
Like sharks, we can't chew. We rip off bits of body and gulp them down.

Sometimes we leave the body to rot until it's soft and squishy enough to bite off bits more easily.

The acid in our stomach is strong enough to dissolve bones.

Hey – why's that crocodile getting all the attention?

Cos he's more interesting than you!

And now for the disgusting details that you'll probably wish you hadn't read before supper. At least one chewed-up croc victim was still alive when he was left to rot and he managed to get away. But most victims are dead and end up being dissolved by the croc's super-strong stomach juices. When crocs have been cut open, all that remains of some victims are their finger and toenails. Well, it's good to know crocs don't chew their nails…

Bet you never knew!
Some people in history quite liked crocs. Is that mad or what?
1 In the 1860s King Litunga Sipopa of Barotseland in Africa enjoyed feeding crocs with executed criminals. You could say "Cruel king's cross crocs crunched crooks' corpses" – but I bet you can't say that with a mouthful of people, er, I mean popcorn.

2 *The ancient Egyptians worshipped crocs, and a crocodile-headed monster named Ammut gobbled up the hearts of bad people in the land of the dead. Of course crocs gobbled good people in the land of the living too.*

WELCOME TO THE LAND OF THE DEAD... HOW DID YOU DIE?

I WAS EATEN BY A CROC!

Mind you, most people aren't too fond of crocs. And many human-killing crocs are hunted, killed and even eaten. Can you believe that crocodile tastes like a cross between fish and beef? I bet you could even make one into a fishcake-flavoured beefburger!

Bet you never knew!
In 1995 a pair of crocs were blamed for eating children in Cameroon, Africa. The wretched reptiles were dressed up as humans – complete with silly wigs – and burnt alive.

More often crocs and alligators are hunted for their skins and have ended up as posh shoes and handbags. By the 1960s nearly all the alligators in the USA had been wiped out by hunters. So does that mean that crocs are out of the running for the Cruellest Creature Competition? Are we more of a danger to them than they are to us?

We've just had another late entry to the competition...

NAME OF CREATURE: Komodo dragon

TYPE OF ANIMAL: Reptile (to be more exact, it's a giant monitor lizard)

DIET: Carnivore. Eats anything it can sink its jaws into. It's especially keen on wild boar and deer but it'll happily munch on us.

NUMBER OF PEOPLE KILLED: They eat a tourist every few years.

WHERE THEY LIVE: A few islands in Indonesia including Komodo.

SIZE: About 2.6 metres long.

FEARSOME FEATURES:

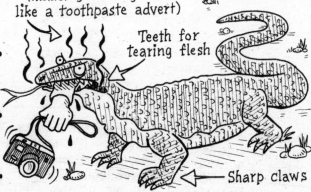

Disgusting bad breath (makes your dog look like a toothpaste advert)

Teeth for tearing flesh

Sharp claws

So, could killer komodo dragons be crueller than crafty
crocodiles? Whilst we're waiting for the judges to
decide, here's a problem page for komodo dragons…
Wow – take a look at this. These dragons are really
beastly to each other!

THE DAILY DRAGON
problem page…

Hi!

**Are you a dragon in difficulties?
Why not drop a line to your
favourite animal agony aunt,
Daphne Dragon?**

Dear Daphne
I'm a baby komodo dragon
with a terrible problem.
My parents have bad
breath and they want to
kill me. What should I do?

Little Nipper

Dad

Mum

**Dear Little Nipper
Your problem is
perfectly normal. All
komodo dragons want
to eat their babies
once they leave their
nest. As for the bad
breath – it's healthy
for us dragons to
have loads of germs
in our mouths. They
get into any creature**

we bite and kill them. And we sniff out their rotting bodies (that's why no dragon should ever use mouthwash).
PS If you really don't want to be eaten try hiding in a tree or rolling in poo. The disgusting stink will put your parents off eating you. It worked for me!

Dear Daphne
I've never eaten with other dragons before and I've heard we can eat each other. Are there any table manners I should remember?
Hungry Snapper

Dear Hungry Snapper
Table manners?! You must be choking, er joking! Simply start with the guts, eat fast and don't be fussy. I'm especially fond of an over-ripe deer with a side order of maggots. If you don't like the maggots you can lick them off the meat and if they crawl up your nose you can sneeze them out! Bon appetit!

Well, those dragons sound completely cruel to me … but it looks like the judges disagree!

> ### The Cruellest Creature Competition Judges' Ruling
> Although komodo dragons do kill humans, they don't kill enough people to take part in the competition. The dragons are DISQUALIFIED!
> The Judges

So it's disappointment for the dragons and cheers for the crocs. But are the crocs cruel enough to win the coveted cruel creatures cup? Well, the competition's getting tough. I mean look at the creatures in the next chapter – you can't trust these slippery characters. They're real snakes in the grass. I'm not joking – they really *are* snakes in the grass!

SINISTER SNAKES

Pssst! Listen carefully. Whilst you read this chapter it's best to remain completely still. This chapter is all about the most deadly snakes on the planet, and if you move too fast they might get upset and you'll be hissss-tory. So no fidgeting, OK?

Now it so happens that Honest Bob is writing a best-selling children's book on snakes (well, it's a best-seller according to Bob). But Bob's book isn't exactly truthful – can you spot at least FIVE fibs in it?

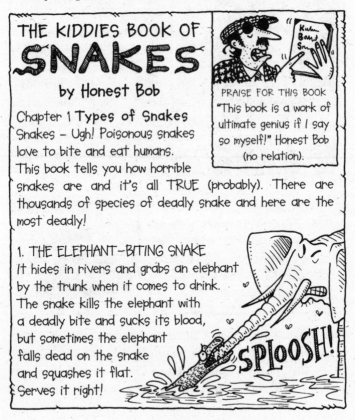

THE KIDDIES BOOK OF
SNAKES
by Honest Bob

PRAISE FOR THIS BOOK
"This book is a work of ultimate genius if I say so myself!" Honest Bob (no relation).

Chapter 1 **Types of Snakes**
Snakes – Ugh! Poisonous snakes love to bite and eat humans. This book tells you how horrible snakes are and it's all TRUE (probably). There are thousands of species of deadly snake and here are the most deadly!

1. THE ELEPHANT–BITING SNAKE
It hides in rivers and grabs an elephant by the trunk when it comes to drink. The snake kills the elephant with a deadly bite and sucks its blood, but sometimes the elephant falls dead on the snake and squashes it flat. Serves it right!

SPLOOSH!

2. THE HOOP SNAKE

This American snake grips its tail in its mouth and rolls along like a hoop. There's no hoop of escaping it! As my old mum says, "what goes around comes around!"

3. THE COACHWHIP SNAKE

If the hoop snake doesn't get you, the coachwhip will. This American snake gallops faster than a horse. And when it catches you, it wraps its body around you and whips you to death with its tail.

Take it from me, kids, the best thing to do with snakes is to kill them stone dead before they kill you even more stony dead. But BEWARE – their mate will try to kill you in revenge!

OH NO! I've haven't read so much rubbish since *Teachers Are Nice to Their Pupils* by Biggy Lyer. So how many fibs, porkies and whoppers did you spot? Why not re-read Bob's book and double-check before reading on?

We wanted to ask Bob about the fibs in his book but he's gone for a long holiday in Peru. Oh well, at least Bob's book shows us some of the barmy beliefs that people have about snakes. In a moment we'll be finding out real-life poisonous snake secrets, but first let's meet a ruthless reptile that likes to get wrapped up in its work…

Sickening squeezers

Some snakes, such as boa constrictors and pythons, wrap themselves around their victims. Will is showing Mickey how an African rock python attacks its prey. Take care, Will!

Will D Beest in … Python pressure

Will's in a tight spot…

I think we'd better move on swiftly to somewhere a bit safer… Oh dear, this page isn't safer at all!

Angry animals fact file

NAME OF CREATURE: King cobra

TYPE OF ANIMAL: Reptile

DIET: Carnivore. Eats other snakes and lizards.

FEARSOME FEATURES:

Poison glands in head make poison.

Flexible jaws for swallowing victim whole.

Neck widens to warn off larger creatures.

HMMM — WONDER WHAT MONKEY TASTES LIKE…

Fangs inject poison.

Tongue tastes scents in the air.

Leathery waterproof eggs. (All snakes produce eggs but some keep them in their bodies until the babies hatch.)

Body senses sound waves through the ground (snakes don't have ears).

NUMBER OF PEOPLE KILLED: The total number of people killed by all types of snakes could be as high as 60,000 per year. Many of them are killed by cobras! Oh yikes!

WHERE THEY LIVE: India and south-east Asia.

SIZE: Up to 5.6 metres long.

Bet you never knew!

So you thought cobras were bad news? Pah – you haven't lived! And you won't live long either if you get too close to a pit viper. Unlike cobras, the vicious vipers (such as rattlesnakes) have heat-sensing pits on their heads to find you in the dark. And they have hollow fangs to inject larger and more deadly doses of poison. (In cobras and most other snakes the poison runs along grooves – but that doesn't mean a cobra bite is "groovy".)

Ruthless relatives

Here are a few more poisonous snakes you wouldn't want to wake up with…

Common krait (12 other species)
Size: Up to 1.8 metres long.
Lives: India and southern Asia.
Danger-rating: The Indian common krait likes nothing better than crawling into your bed whilst you're asleep. Unfortunately its bite contains a deadly nightmare nerve poison… Sweet dreams!

A CRATE OF KRAITS

Rattlesnake

Size: Up to 2.4 metres (eastern diamondback).
Lives: North America.
Danger-rating: There are 29 species

and they're all poisonous. They kill fewer than 15 people in the USA every year, though.

Sea snake

Size: Up to 90 cm long.
Lives: Indian and Pacific Oceans.
Danger-rating: Rarely bites humans although it does enjoy chasing divers. Its bite is the most poisonous of any snake. Fancy a dip?

Black mamba

Size: Up to 4.3 metres long.
Lives: Africa south of the Sahara Desert.
Danger-rating: Its poison can kill in 20 minutes. In the 1970s South African snake expert Jack Seale spent weeks sharing a small room with a black mamba. He said the secret of survival was not to move quickly... Lucky he didn't need the toilet in a hurry then.

The spitting cobra

Size: Up to 2.5 metres long.
Lives: Africa – south of the Sahara desert.
Danger-rating: Low. OK, so if you dried the poison and injected

it into 165 humans they'd all die. But this snake *spits* its poison (how come you knew that already?) and it can't hurt if it lands on your skin. The bad news: if the poison hits your eyes it can dissolve your eyeballs. The very bad news: the snake aims for the eyes. The yikes-I-need-a-clean-pair-of-pants bad news: it's a very good shot.

Dare you discover … if you're as accurate as the spitting cobra?

You will need:

A water pistol (Make sure you fill it with water and not snake poison!)

An eyeball. (If you don't have a spare eyeball here's one we've borrowed. You can trace it and draw it on a piece of card.)

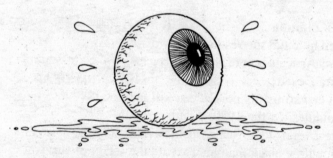

A measuring tape
Blu Tack

HURRY UP – I
NEED IT BACK!

What you do:

1 Stick the eyeball to the wall 1.5 metres up with the Blu Tack (this is best done outside).

2 Measure 2.5 metres from the wall.

3 Crouch down and try to hit the eyeball with a jet of water.

You should find:
This is tricky for you but easy for a sinister spitting cobra,

HORRIBLE HEALTH WARNING!

You should only use water pistols for this experiment and that means NO SPITTING. And no spitting at your pet snake/teacher either!

Is your teacher a herpetologist (that's the posh name for a snake scientist)? If so, they may have a cobra named Colin which they feed small furry animals (so that's what happened to Hamish the school hamster!). Anyway here are some strange snake secrets that they probably don't know…

Seven strange snake secrets

1 Even your most scary school teacher can't out-stare a snake. Snakes can't blink because they don't have eyelids. See-through scales protect their eyes.

2 Ever wondered how sea snakes eat really spiny fish without them getting stuck in their throats? Me neither – but apparently they gulp the fish and then force the spines out through their own bodies. I guess they must be prickly characters!

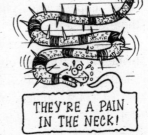

THEY'RE A PAIN IN THE NECK!

3 It's possible to eat snake eggs. The trick is to choose the smooth ones. The crumpled ones contain baby snakes and their bite can be poisonous. So if you eat the wrong egg you'd best scramble.

4 Although snakes taste smells using their tongues, some species have nostrils too.

5 Snakes take baths. Before they shed their skin they take a dip to make the skin moist. Then they unroll their skin along the length of their body. It's a bit like Will D Beest taking off a sock – but without the cheesy whiff.

PHWOAR!

6 A snake can decide how much poison to give you. The crosser the snake the more you get!

7 And talking about poison, US scientists have found that cottonmouth snake poison is ideal for shifting stubborn stains. Of course it shifts stubborn humans too. Anyone want to test the vile venomous cleaner? If the test goes wrong at least you'd suffer a clean death.

Strange snake scientists

Snake experts are trying strange snake experiments all the time…

• Kenyan-based fang fancier Constantine Ionides invented a pair of goggles to protect his eyes from spitting cobra poison, kept a pet puff adder named Popkiss and ate a gaboon viper for Christmas dinner. He even raced a black mamba to find out how fast it was – luckily it proved slower than the barmy boffin.

THEY NEED WINDSCREEN **VIPERS**, MR IONIDES!

• Our old pal Charles Waterton (last seen riding on a crocodile) once let a rattlesnake loose at a scientific meeting. I bet the scared scientists were even more rattled than the rattlesnake.

So it's not too surprising that lots of snake experts have been bitten by the snakes they tried to study. Take John Toomey, for example…

NAME: John Toomey **DATE:** 1916

JOB: Zookeeper at Bronx Zoo, New York

INJURY: Bitten by a rattlesnake

CONDITION: Desperate. Another zookeeper tried to suck out the poison but the swelling has spread all over Toomey's body. He's in extreme pain and throwing up all the time.

MEDICAL FORECAST: He's a goner without a doubt...

NOTES: Toomey's life was saved by Brazilian snake expert Dr Vital Brazil. By an amazing chance, Dr Brazil just happened to be in New York and just happened to have some of his newly invented snakebite remedy with him. Toomey was the first person saved by the cure.

Bet you never knew!
Scientist Karl Schmidt wasn't so lucky. In 1957 he was studying a snake called a boomslang. The bad-tempered boomslang bit careless Karl with just one fang. But the bite was deadly and the suffering scientist died the next day.

A snakebite survivor's story

So, how does it feel to be bitten by a poisonous snake – is it really as bad as it sounds? Well, no. Actually, it's a whole lot WORSE!

In 1987 British snake expert Jack Corney (1924–2003) was collecting poison from a rattlesnake for scientists to study. Jack knew what he was doing but as he held the snake by the back of its neck the killer creature bit his thumb.

"Don't panic," Jack said to himself grimly. "Freeze your mind." He knew that if he let himself feel scared, his heart would beat faster and pump the poison more quickly around his body.

Carefully he replaced the snake in its box and wrapped a bandage tightly around his bitten arm. But he was too late. As the poison took hold Jack began to gasp for air. His injured arm swelled to three times its size. The pain was an unspeakable agony. Jack gritted his teeth and rang for help.

In hospital Jack's heart stopped, but he still could hear and feel as the doctors fought for his life. One doctor held Jack's wrist and tried to find a pulse as another stuck a needle in his arm.

"We're losing him," said one doctor.

"He's gone."

Jack felt as if he was drifting out of his body. Then everything went black.

Suddenly Jack's eyes opened. He was looking at a clock. Where was he? What had happened? Slowly and painfully he realized that he was still in hospital and three hours had passed. He later found out that his heart had stopped for three minutes and it had only started to beat again at the last moment before death. For five days he was more dead than alive, and even when he began to get better his arm was useless for weeks. Then Jack went back to work studying snakes.

He was bitten several times after that. Ten years later Jack remarked…

"Some people think I'm mad doing this job…"

Now I wonder why they thought that?

Obviously you don't want to mess about with poisonous snakes – so here are a few snake experts' safety tips, just in case you find yourself in snake country…

Expert snake safety tips - don't leave home without them!

1. Always wear long trousers and boots. They protect you against bites from small snakes!

2. Always step on top of logs rather than over them. There may be a snake hiding on the other side.

3. If you see a snake always keep a safe distance - the snake can't strike more than half its length.

4. Make sure the snake has a way to escape.

5. Stay calm - I said DON'T PAAAAAAANIC!

Hmm, poisonous snakes certainly sound like the odds-on favourites for the Cruellest Creature Competition. They kill more humans than sharks and one snake even shot a man... Well, I don't care if you don't believe me – IT'S TRUE!

Bet you never knew!
In June 1996 a Chinese hunter named Li from Shanxi Province was feeling bored. He came across a snake and thought it might be fun to prod it with his gun. The surprised snake coiled around the gun, pulled the trigger and blasted Li in the bum. He died soon afterwards ... shot by a snake!

Mind you, the Cruellest Creature Competition is still wide open and our next cruel chapter features a creature that's horribly big, scoffs buns and lets out loud trumpets. And NO – I'm not talking about your teacher!

BIG BAD BEASTS

I'm delighted to tell you that Will D Beest has almost recovered from his unfortunate encounter with the python. And here he is to introduce this chapter…

As a famous TV personality I get many invitations…

OH GET ON WITH IT!

Yes, please do…

Plant-eaters can be just as deadly as meat-eaters.

That's true — I could murder a banana!

Thank you, Will. The first animal we'll be looking at is a creature that kills hundreds of people every year. It's a jumbo-sized menace…

Angry animals fact file

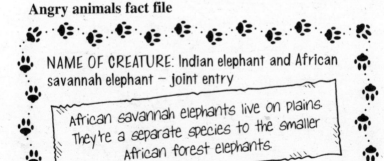

NAME OF CREATURE: Indian elephant and African savannah elephant — joint entry

African savannah elephants live on plains. They're a separate species to the smaller African forest elephants.

TYPE OF ANIMAL: Mammal

DIET: Herbivore. Elephants eat just about any plant food...

• They pull up grass with their trunks and uproot trees, eating everything including the bark and roots.

• Elephants can guzzle more than 200 kg of greenery a day, so imagine what a herd of elephants would do to your school cabbage patch.

NUMBER OF PEOPLE KILLED: Evil elephants kill about 200 people in India alone. But savannah elephants are worse-tempered.

FEARSOME FEATURES:

OOER!

SAVANNAH ELEPHANT

Trunk = the elephant's nose and upper lip, used for drinking, sniffing and picking things up.

Tough, leathery skin.

Smaller ears than African elephants.

"Lip" on upper end of trunk is handy for holding small objects.

Tusks = extra-long front teeth used for digging for food and fighting. (Female Indian elephants don't have tusks.)

INDIAN ELEPHANT

WHERE THEY LIVE: The Indian elephant lives in India (oddly enough) and South-east Asia. And I bet you'll be trumpeting with amazement to read that both types of African elephant live in Africa, south of the Sahara Desert.

SIZE: Indian elephant: up to 3 metres high at the shoulder.
Savannah elephant: up to 3.2 metres high at the shoulder.

Extreme elephant attacks

In 1952 a hunter named JC Hunter (no, I'm not making this up as I go along) said: "I have often been chased by elephants. It is like running from a nightmare … not a second goes by but you expect to feel that snaking trunk round your neck."

And when the elephant catches you, things get far, far worse – but I'm sure you won't want to read these upsetting details…

OH YES WE DO!

Well don't say I didn't warn you! The elephant picks up the human with its trunk and throws them to the ground or bashes their brains out against a tree. And then the enraged elephant splats them flat with its big heavy feet. I think you'll agree that's a nasty way to *goo*.

WHAT'S THAT SMELL?

SNIFF!

I TROD ON SOMEONE NASTY.

71

People who train elephants have to be extra careful, because the big brutal beasts get angry without warning. In the 1900s an elephant named Mandarin performed in a US circus. One day a new trainer started work. Mandarin had been taught to place his foot on the previous trainer's head. But guess what happened when the new trainer tried that trick?

Bet you never knew!
A US circus elephant that killed a cruel trainer in 1916 was hanged by the neck until she was dead. It's said that the elephant's owners tried to electrocute her but the jumbo-sized shock just left her a bit dazed.

So are you a cool clued-up elephant expert who'd know what to do if an elephant decided to pay your school an unfriendly visit? Or would you be cowering in a cupboard along with your terrified teacher? Try our teasing quiz and find out!

Could you be an elephant expert?
Which of the two possible answers is correct? You've got a one in two chance of being right so it's OK to guess!

1 How can you tell when an elephant is growing up?

a) Its voice breaks.

b) It gets spotty and wants to stay out late.

2 Older elephants suffer from worn teeth. Because they can't eat too easily they get hungry and grumpy and violent. What did Thai scientist Dr Somsak Jitniyom give Morokot the toothless elephant in 2004?

a) False teeth.

b) Milkshakes.

3 How do farmers in Zimbabwe stop elephants from eating their crops?

a) They pay boys to throw stones at them.

b) They burn a mixture of chilli and elephant poo.

4 Why did elephants flatten an Indian army base in 1996?

a) They jumped up and down on an ants' nest and the ground shook so much the buildings fell down.

b) They got drunk.

Answers:

1 a) Austrian scientists found this out in 2003.

2 a) Yes – it's a CHEW story!

3 b) Elephants sniff out crops 10 km away. The terrible tuskers march in and munch the lot, and the poor farmers starve. But the spicy stink of chilli and poo puts them off. Believe it or not, elephants hate chilli and that's why you'll never find an elephant in a Mexican restaurant. By the way, throwing stones at an elephant is even less sensible than using a python as a skipping rope.

4 b) They were drunk on rotting fruit that contained alcohol. When the boozy beasts raided the camp's drink store a brave soldier tried to stop them, but they flattened his hut. The answer can't be **a)** because elephants can't jump.

I SAID, **HALT!**

WHAT YOUR SCORE MEANS…

4 CONGRATULATIONS – you're an excellent elephant expert and I bet you've got a jumbo-sized brain!

2–3 You might get into a flap if an elephant flapped its ears at you.

0–1 Oh dear – you'd best keep away from elephants. So where's the nearest cupboard?

Mind you, if elephants can be evil you might think these horrible herbivores are worse. Read on now and decide which is cruellest – the terrible tuskers, battering buffalo or horrible hippos…

Battering buffalo

Cowboys call them "buffalo", but actually they're North American bison. Whatever they are, they're awesomely powerful beasts. A male bison can be 2 metres high from the top of its hump and twice as long, and its skull is even thicker than a school bully's. The skull's said to be bullet-proof (and it's certainly bully-proof)…

Although buffalo rarely kill humans, they will fight back if they think they're being attacked. In 1799 US farmer Samuel McClellan shot at a herd of buffalo that had invaded his farm. The buffalo were starving because humans had taken their grazing land. When Sam stupidly stabbed the leading male buffalo the others overran his house and flattened his family. There's a famous old song that goes…

Oh give me a home where the buffalo roam!

But I don't think that's what it meant. And I don't suppose the buffaloes wiped their feet either…

Bet you never knew!

US General George A Custer (1839–1876) is famous for being killed by Native Americans at the Battle of Little Big Horn. But a few years earlier Custer was nearly killed by the big horn of a buffalo instead. He was out hunting when a brave bison attacked him. The gun-toting general panicked and shot his own horse. Hmm – he sounds like a cowardly Custer to me.

Hair-raising hippos (or hippopotami if you want to wake everyone up in science class)

We're going to find out what makes these angry animals awesomely awful by letting loose a herd of them in a school swimming pool...

You can see what makes a hippo such a menace if you peer into its giant gob.

WOW! It's the biggest yawn of any animal — even bigger than when I nod off in Mr Bottomly's biology class!

50-cm-long teeth

Baby hippos are born underwater

SNORE~GLUG GLUG!

Hippos snooze underwater and come up for air in their sleep.

And if those teeth look scary, worse is still to come – a hippo has an even more vicious temper than a teacher on a wet Monday morning. And to make matters worse humans are *always* upsetting them.

• People don't spot the hippo snoozing in the river and whack it on the nose with their canoe paddles.

• People don't spot the hippo feeding on land at night and bump into it. The trouble is, an angry hippo can run faster than a human!

Either way, the result is a dreadful death for the human. And horrible hippos kill more people than lions and elephants put together.

Bet you never knew!
In 2002 a hippo-attack victim arrived in hospital in Zululand, South Africa. His whole face had been bitten off and all that was left was one eyeball. Incredibly, the patient doctors called "the miracle man" survived the attack.

Well, if you ask me the evil elephants or horrible hippos could win by a short head or even a long trunk… But the creature lurking in the next chapter could be even worse. If you go down to the woods today you're sure of a *horrible* surprise. Let's take a peek through the keyhole…

ER – HAS ANYONE GOT ANY HONEY?

BEWARE OF THE BEARS

Mr Bottomly has a deeply embarrassing secret…

Mr Bottomly by day

The bear is a crepuscular omnivore, blah, blah…

bear

Mr Bottomly by night

Night, night, Mr Wuffles

Oh dear, this is shocking – but a lot of people honestly think bears are cute cuddly teddies. Huh! If you tried to cuddle a real bear you'd suffer a grisly grizzly fate…

Angry animals fact file

NAME OF CREATURE: Brown bear (known in North America as the grizzly)

TYPE OF ANIMAL: Mammal

DIET: Bears are omnivores and insectivores. They eat everything – and I mean EVERYTHING! If you don't believe me, just wait 'til you get to page 87!

NUMBER OF PEOPLE KILLED: Less than five a year in the USA.

WHERE THEY LIVE: Wild areas of North America, Russia and Eastern Europe.

SIZE: About 1.3 metres to their big hairy shoulders.

FEARSOME FEATURES: Sense of smell is 100 times more sensitive than a human's.

Coat can be brown... or black or even blond. (Best not ask this grizzly if she's a "natural blonde".)

Grumpy bad temper.

GRRR!

"Hump" on back called a roach.

Different types of teeth for biting and slicing meat and chewing plant food.

14-cm claws.

Grizzlies can have two or three cubs every three years.

Powerful legs can run at 50 km per hour.

Ruthless relatives

Black bear
Size: Up to 1.7 metres long (they're smaller than brown bears).
Lives: North American forests.
Danger-rating: They kill a human every five years or so. Because they often live closer to humans they attack us more often than brown bears

... AND WE'RE "TREE-MENDOUS" CLIMBERS!

Polar bear

Size: Up to 3 metres tall on their hind legs. Polar bears are the biggest meat-eaters on land. (If you meet one in the dark it won't be all white on the night.)

Lives: On and around the Arctic Ocean.

OF COURSE WE'RE THE BIGGEST MEAT-EATERS... THERE AREN'T ANY PLANTS!

Danger-rating: On average, polar bears kill a person every three years or so in North America. They kill even more rarely in Russia.

We fitted Will D Beest and Mickey with centrally-heated thermal pants and sent them off to check out the dangers...

Will D Beest in ... Polar peril

I'm starring in this Arctic adventure!

IT'S PANTS!

Polar bears ambush seals when they come up to breathe...

B-b-b-b

SEAL BREATHING HOLE

Oh dear! Looks like Will's in a hole lot of bother. He'll bear-ly escape with his life, but he's bear-ing up well, and bear-ing in mind… (Aggggh! I can't bear these bear jokes – The Editor.) Anyway, Will was so busy being mugged by the bear that he forgot to tell us that bears prefer scoffing seals to people. You see, seals have more juicy, energy-rich fat – or blubber – than us…

So I guess we humans aren't filling enough for them…

Talking about polar bears, did you know that they're all left-handed? Or did I make that up? Your teacher might know – so here's your chance to torture your teacher with a queasy quiz featuring all kinds of bears (it's purely in the interests of entertainment – I mean education!).

Teacher's terror torture test

Test rules

1 The answers to this quiz are either TRUE or FALSE.

2 They're designed to be incredibly hard.

3 If you're soppily soft-hearted you can let your teacher ask the class before he decides...

4 For every wrong answer your teacher loses a point.

5 Whenever his score totals ZERO or less he has to sit on a giant whoopee farting cushion.

True or false?

1 Polar bears are left-handed.

 **2** In 2003 a polar bear in a zoo in Argentina was dyed pink.

IT MADE ME SEE RED!

3 Bear brains have a built-in cooling system.

IT'S IMPORTANT TO KEEP A COOL HEAD!

4 Bears don't go to the toilet all winter.

ROLL ON THE SPRING!

5 Some bears pee whilst doing handstands.

OK SO I HAVEN'T GOT THE HANG OF IT YET!

6 Brown bears stink of rotten fish.

YOU DON'T SMELL TOO GOOD YOURSELF!

7 The best thing to do if you're attacked by a brown bear is climb a tree.

ANYONE GOT A LADDER?

84

Answers:

1 TRUE – polar bears probably shake hands with their left paws, but other bears can be left- or right-handed.

2 FALSE – pink polar bears, ha ha – as if! No, the polar bear was dyed *purple* by an antiseptic spray. Now isn't that a colour to "dye" for?

3 TRUE – the blood vessel that goes to the brain is designed to lose heat to cooler veins heading in the opposite direction. Hot-headed bears also lose heat through their noses.

4 TRUE – bears don't poo or pee for six months when they're hibernating (sleeping through the winter). So how long can your teacher last? Hmm – on second thoughts, don't ask!

5 TRUE – pandas pee on trees to mark their territory. Standing on its front paws helps the panda pee higher and so fool other pandas that it's bigger. Don't try handstands in the toilet – they can result in unfortunate accidents!

6 FALSE – they have a kind of soggy doggy smell.

7 TRUE – but only if it's an adult bear. Their claws are the wrong shape for climbing.

So how did your teacher get on? If he lost he'll be in a beastly bad-temper as he bounces on the farting cushion like a kangaroo fed on beans. But if he won he could be a secret bear boffin and he won't be too miffed when you take your pet bear to school. "Pet *bear*?" I hear you ask. Why yes – here's how to look after one…

THE HORRIBLE SCIENCE Bear Care Guide

It's great being a baby-bear owner. Just follow our advice for hours of bear fun and games!

Lesson 1 Bear bed-time

It helps to stay awake at the same time as your bear. Your bear is crepuscular (that's a posh word meaning active at dawn and dusk) and you'll have to be too. So you'll have an early start - yawn! But if you get tired you can always take an afternoon nap in your science lesson!

SORRY, MISS, BUT I'M CREPUSCULAR!

Lesson 2 Making your bear feel at home

Don't expect your bear to help with the housework. If it's as badly behaved as the naughty black bears that break into homes in the wilds of North America,

IT WASN'T ME, MUM!

it'll smash all the china, leave muddy paw-prints everywhere and poo in your brother's bed. Your family might be a bit put out and your bear might be put out too. That's put outside to sleep, and you'll be sent to join it. Oh well, wild bears sleep on a bed of leaves and moss and they're comfy enough!

Lesson 3 Feeding your bear

Like all mammals, baby bears drink their mum's gloopy milk. But when it's four months old, your bear cub will want to sample adult bear foods such as...

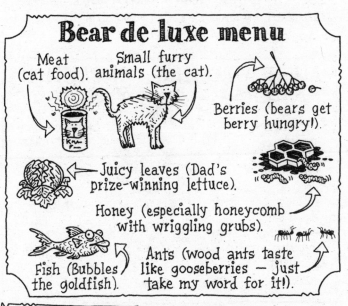

Bear de-luxe menu

Meat (cat food).

Small furry animals (the cat).

Berries (bears get berry hungry!).

Juicy leaves (Dad's prize-winning lettuce).

Honey (especially honeycomb with wriggling grubs).

Fish (Bubbles the goldfish).

Ants (wood ants taste like gooseberries — just take my word for it!).

During the building of the Trans-canada highway, bears raided the builders' stores. The greedy grizzlies actually ate dynamite, but DON'T try feeding your bear on explosives!

Lesson 4 School-time is play-time!

Your bear is sure to rule the school. All your friends will want to pet your pet and give it their unwanted school dinners (yes, bears really do eat anything). And it's bound to be very educational when your bear trashes the classroom. I'm sure your teacher will want to join in the fun by being chased round the football pitch and having his bottom whacked by the bear's paw ... followed by a spot of bear wrestling!

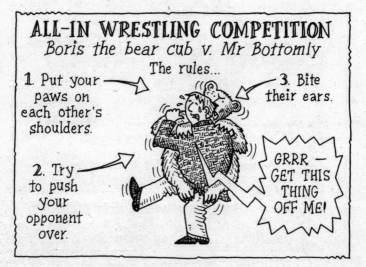

ALL-IN WRESTLING COMPETITION
Boris the bear cub v. Mr Bottomly

The rules...

1. Put your paws on each other's shoulders.

3. Bite their ears.

2. Try to push your opponent over.

GRRR — GET THIS THING OFF ME!

Of course this is all harmless fun. But you'd better stop your bear behaving as badly as black bears in US National Parks...

• Jumping on car roofs to break open the door and steal food.

• Chasing people with food until they panic and drop it – and then scoffing it!

BLACK BEAR

NO YOU CAN'T HAVE MY STICKY BUN!

After a day of bear fun your teacher's sure to be in a good mood. In fact he'll probably reward you and your pet with a long holiday! This is also known as "being expelled".

Lesson 5 A nice long rest

Your bear will get sleepy in the autumn and want to hibernate all winter. Simply help your bear dig a huge sleeping den in the garden. I'm sure your dad will be delighted if you dig up his boring old prize-winning vegetables ... and if you're still banned from the house you could always move in with your bear! There's only one problem – bears snore! Oh well, you'll just have to grin and BEAR it!

SNORRRE!

A rather-too-late warning from the author

Baby bears are dangerous. They're strong enough to hurt people and trash your home, and you shouldn't have one as a pet. It's lucky you didn't take our Bear Care Guide too seriously!

Oh you did? And you're sending me the bill? Gulp – I'm off to join Honest Bob in Peru!

Bet you never knew!
In the 1990s a Hungarian couple bought a cute white puppy. They became a bit worried when their pet grew very big and smashed up their home. And they were even more alarmed to discover their puppy was really a polar bear!

GRRR!

ER... WALKIES?

But if baby bears can do dreadful things to your furniture, just think what an adult bear could do to YOU! I mean, look at what happened to poor old Hugh Glass. In 1823 Hugh was part of an expedition exploring the wilds of North America…

My Diary by Hugh Glass
August 1823

I'm in a mess. I'm covered in scratches and my leg is broken. I guess it was my fault. I should never have gone into the forest by myself. I never meant to go disturb that mother bear, but she thought I was hunting her cub and attacked me. I had to kill her – but she darn near killed me first…

One week later

All the others have gone but John Fitzgerald and Jim Bridger were left behind to look after me ... until I die. I heard them last night. John was whispering that I was a goner and all they had to do was sneak off and say I was already dead.

← J.B.
← J.F.

One day later...

When I woke up this morning, John and Jim were gone. They've taken all my belongings.

"Grr – I ain't finished yet!" I told myself angrily.

So I put a splint on my broken leg and wrapped myself in the bear's skin. My wounds were so rotten I had to roll in maggots. The hungry little varmints ate the bad bits off me. Then I began to crawl. I'm heading for Fort Kiowa – but it's 320 kilometres. Will I make it?

CHOMP!

GASP!

Eight weeks later...

I'm STARVING. I've been living off rotten dead buffalo and berries and snakes, but I won't give up. Some days the pain drives me crazy. If I ever find that John and Jim I'LL KILL THE PAIR OF THEM! That's if I live that long! I've just reached the Cheyenne River and I've just about reached the end of my tether... What now???

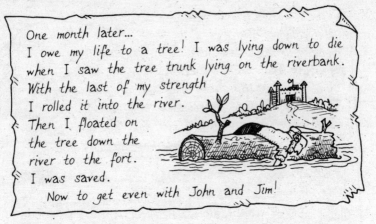

One month later...

I owe my life to a tree! I was lying down to die when I saw the tree trunk lying on the riverbank. With the last of my strength I rolled it into the river. Then I floated on the tree down the river to the fort. I was saved.

Now to get even with John and Jim!

You'll be pleased to hear that when Hugh Glass caught up with John and Jim he forgave them. In fact Hugh was lucky. Lucky to find his way to safety and even more lucky to survive the bear's attack. A bear can kill a human with a blow of its paw – and it all takes less than 30 seconds.

Could you be a scientist?

In 1984 US scientist Doug Dunbar sprayed a new anti-bear pepper spray in a bear's face. What happened?

a) The angry animal chewed up the scientist.
b) Nothing. The bear simply walked away.
c) The angry animal sneezed bear-snot all over the scientist.

ACHOO!

UGH! IT'S YOGI, I MEAN, **BOGEY** BEAR!

Answer:
a) Mind you, it took a few tries before the scientist made a bear angry enough to attack and test the spray. Before then the bears wandered off, so there's half a point for b).

92

So, bears are quite hard to annoy, it seems. That's interesting. Could it be that bear attacks aren't always the bear's fault? Could humans be to blame? Consider these facts: rangers in Yellowstone Park, USA, once stopped a woman dabbing honey on her child's face so a bear could lick it off. Another man put a bear in his car to take a photo of it sitting next to his wife. So who was more brainless – the humans or the bears? We've asked a brainy bear to explain the bear's point of view to a rather brainless human...

Bear's
point of view

 Human's
point of view

You disturb us when we're resting and frighten our cubs.

You act like bears with sore heads!

You humans take our territories to graze your animals.

You bears eat our animals.

Then you shoot us!

Hey, lighten up, buddy! It's only sport! You bears steal our food.

So maybe bears aren't so cruel?

Maybe they're not even front-runners for the Cruellest Creature Competition?

What do *you* think?

Tell you what – you can always make up your mind after the next chapter. Now – who's brave enough to feed our next group of angry animals? Oh thanks, Will!

CRUEL BIG CATS

Please answer the following questions...

1 Do you live with a cat?

2 Does your cat enjoy playing with half-dead mice, staring hungrily at the budgie and sinking her claws into the postman?

If you answered "yes" to both of the above questions it's quite likely that you own a cruel cat. But even the cruellest cat is a cutesy-pie kitten compared to this lot...

No wonder they didn't want the cat food. Er, has anyone seen Will?

Angry animals fact file

NAME OF CREATURE: Tiger and lion – joint entry

We're looking at both animals because they both kill lots of people.

TYPE OF ANIMAL: Mammal

DIET: Meat, meat and more meat – ideally large four-footed creatures. Lions like wildebeest and zebra. Tigers eat several species of Indian deer. Oh yes, and neither species minds munching a human...

NUMBER OF PEOPLE KILLED: Each year lions kill hundreds of people in Africa and tigers kill over 100 people in India.

WHERE THEY LIVE: Lions live on open plains in Africa (with a few in India). Tigers live in forests, mainly in India and Nepal with a few in South-east Asia, China and Russia.

SIZE: Lions and tigers grow up to 2.7 metres long including their tails.

FEARSOME FEATURES:

Paws the size of a man's head.

LION

Greasy waterproof coat.

Canine teeth for biting prey.

Claws as thick as a man's thumb for pulling down prey.

GRRR!

Flesh-slicing back teeth.

TIGER

Slightly bulging eyes for all-round vision.

Stripy coat to blend in with long grass and forest.

Soft paws for silent creeping.

Ruthless relatives

Although lions and tigers look different, they're part of
the same group of animals – scientists call them the
Panthera, or roaring cats. (Your cat isn't a roaring cat –
she's a mewing cat. Especially when she wants more
supper and she's trying to make you feel sorry for her.)
But here's some roaring panthera you really wouldn't
want to meet on a dark night…

Jaguar

Size: Up to 1.9 metres long.
Lives: Forests in South America.
Danger-rating: Rarely attacks
humans but does enjoy sinking its
fangs into a victim's brain. Maybe
it's hungry for knowledge…

Puma (alias the cougar or
mountain lion and I bet if
one attacked you, you might
like to call it other names).
Size: Up to 2.4 metres long.
Lives: Wild parts of
North and South America.
Danger-rating: Can attack people but deaths are very rare.

Leopard

GRRR — WHERE'S THE MONKEY FROM PAGE 94?

Size: Up to 2.5 metres long (including tail).

Lives: Plains in Africa and forests in India.

Danger-rating: They normally hunt monkeys and antelopes 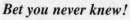 but they have a horribly antisocial habit of breaking into huts and grabbing people in their sleep. I guess if the spotted cat spots you, you'll be in a tight spot.

> *Bet you never knew!*
> In 1998 a puma calmly strolled into the office of a plastics company in the USA. It scared the secretaries and terrified the typists until a brave employee locked it in an empty office. Well, I hope the office was empty…
>
> GOOD DAY AT THE OFFICE, DEAR?

As you've just found out lions and tigers live in different places, but let's imagine a lion cub and tiger cub met for a chat. OK, I realize this is going to take a bit of imagining…

Tiger cub — HELLO!   Lion cub — HI!

TC: Mum feeds me.

LC: Mum and Gran and Mum's sisters feed me. We're called a pride – well, Mum's proud of us!

TC: We only feed every few days.

LC: So do we – blimey I'm starving!

TC: Mum lets me eat first.

LC: Huh – you're lucky! I have to eat last.

TC: I never see my dad.

LC: My dad rules the pride.

TC: My mum made a chemical message in her wee to attract my dad.

LC: So did my mum. Grown-ups are s-o-o disgusting!

TC: My dad makes a Aoooom! sound to warn off other tigers.

LC: My dad roars.

TC: If a new male tiger takes over my dad's territory he could kill me.

LC: If a new male takes over the pride he could kill me.

 WE HAVE IT TOUGH!

TC: Fancy a game of chase?

LC: OK – you're IT!

Actually, lion and tiger cubs don't play for fun. Well, that's according to boring old scientists who haven't had fun for 50 years. Instead, the scientists say the cubs are practising adult skills such as hunting and fighting. Sadly, human cubs aren't allowed to practise vital fighting skills with their brothers and sisters.

And talking about hunting, there was an awful lot of that going on in Tsavo, Africa, in 1898. In that year a pair of man-eating lions ate more than 130 African and Indian workers who were building a railway. Here's how one of the workers might have described the danger. Read on if you think you're up to scratch…

30 November 1898

My dear sister

Here I am in Tsavo, helping to build a railway - but there's a terrible problem. Many of my friends have been eaten by a pair of lions. All we hear is a scream in the night followed by the sound of crunching bones, and in the morning all that's left is a head … or a hand and puddles of blood.

Our boss Colonel Patterson built thorn hedges around the camp and posted guards. But the lions are as fearless as demons. My friends whisper that the lions can't be killed - they call them The Ghost and The Darkness. We were so scared that we took to sleeping in a tree. But we were too heavy and now the tree's fallen down! I'm really scared I'll be the next victim…

Pray for me!

Your brother, Govinder

100

30 December 1898

My dear sister

Much has happened since my last letter. Colonel Patterson built a giant wooden trap and caught one lion.

But some policemen who were helping him tried to shoot the animal. They shot off the lock by mistake and the lion got away!

Then Colonel Patterson's boss came to see what was happening and the lion attacked him and tore up his best suit. This big boss was not happy, especially when the lions ate his pet goats (all except one which the Colonel shot by mistake).

GRRR!

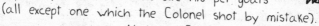

Next the Colonel built a wobbly platform from sticks. He told us he would wait on top of it every night until he could shoot the lions. A few nights later a lion showed up but just then an owl landed on the Colonel's head. The Colonel still managed to fire his gun and hit the lion. He was most pleased. Yesterday the Colonel was even more pleased after he tracked down and shot the second lion.

We workers are happy too because we no longer have to fall asleep wondering whether we will wake up in the lion's jaws. Hooray for Colonel Patterson! I think we all deserve a holiday!

I PROPPED THE DEAD LION UP WITH STICKS!

Your brother,
Govinder

101

Of course there are still man-eating big cats in Africa, and Will wants to find out what it's like to be attacked by one. Crumbs – he must be mad! Remember this?

Will D Beest in … Big cat, BIGGER trouble

SCIENTIFIC NOTE
Leopards drag their victims up a tree so that lions or hyenas can't scoff the body...

This opens up a big ugly can of worms... Why do lions, tigers and leopards attack us? Is it because they don't like us? The answer is NO – or as a scientist would put it...

The main reason why big cats eat us is because they're hungry and we're easy to catch. They could be hungry because...

• They're too old and toothless to catch their usual prey.
• They have been injured in fights with other animals or humans.
• Humans have driven away their usual prey in order to graze their farm animals.

In other words it could be our fault if a big cat turns to eating people. But just to complicate the picture…
• Not all big cats eat people – even if they're hungry.
• Some big cats eat people when they're not obviously starving.
• Some female man-eating big cats train their cubs to eat people too.

And now for a few purr-fectly horrible big cat stories…

Five beastly big cat bites
1 When a tiger grabbed elephant driver Subedar Ali, the young man prayed to all the gods he could think of. The tiger ripped flesh from the top of Ali's head and nearly bit his fingers off. But Ali's elephant picked him up in its trunk and pulled him to safety. Officials at the Corbett National Park, India, wanted to shoot the tiger but Ali begged for the animal to be saved. His wish was granted. The tiger was sent to a zoo and Subedar Ali visited it to say "hello".
2 In 1870 James Robinson's Circus visited Middletown, Missouri, in the USA. A ten-piece band played a cheery tune on top of the lions' cage. But the roof was weak. With a bang and a crash the band fell into the lions' cage and seven of them were eaten. So I guess the lions got a taste for music…

DROP IN ANYTIME!

3 In 1937 an English vicar called Harold Davidson was sitting in a cage with a lion named Freddie. (The vicar was trying to make some money after losing his job.) But when the clumsy cleric trod on his tail, Freddie began to feast on the priest with fatal results.

4 Despite the danger, thousands of people keep big cats as pets. In Brazil they're kept as guard dogs – er, cats – and burglars have been eaten. (I wonder if they were beefy burglars, cheesy burglars or even veggie burglars.)

5 In 2003 a man in New York kept a tiger, an alligator and a kitten as pets. But the tiger decided to eat the kitten. The oddball owner tried to save the kitten and got bitten. The big animals ended up in zoos, the man ended up in hospital, and the kitten ended up in shock.

EATEN B-B-B-Y MY OWN R-R-RELATIVE... F-F-F-F-FREAKY!

Well, it does look as if we humans have made the problem of man-eating worse – so does that mean man-eating big cats aren't cruel creatures? And if they are, could they be more savage than sharks and more sinister than snakes? Or more wicked than the creatures in our next blood-curdling chapter?

Read on for the howl truth…

HOWWWWWL!

IS THAT YOU, WILL?

WICKED WOLVES

Fairy stories are full of wolves dressing up as grannies or scaring little pigs, but real wolves are much more dangerous and far more fearsome. In fact, if you ask me, we've found our Cruellest Creature Competition winner! To prove it, I'm going to turn out the lights and tell you a terrible tale about a werewolf – a human who turned into a wolf. WARNING – this could be a bit scary!

The Horrible Science Book of
SCARY TALES
FOR NASTY BOYS AND GIRLS

The evil wolf-man

Are you sitting uncomfortably? Then I'll begin. A long time ago in the cold, bleak Auvergne Mountains of France there lived a nasty nobleman by the name of Count Vargo. This cruel count enjoyed attacking people for fun and he was so evil that even his own mother didn't have a good word to say about him. One day Count Vargo attacked a young girl. Hearing the girl's screams, her two brothers rushed to her rescue. The lads bravely fought the Count off and as the villain ran away into the forest, one of them cursed him.

"The whole of nature will be against you, Count Vargo!"

The cruel Count merely laughed – but within minutes his laughter turned to a scream of terror. Without warning a huge wolf leapt from the bushes. The fearsome beast seized Count Vargo in its sharp slobbery jaws.

"Help me – save me!" shrieked the Count.

An old man heard the Count's cries and set his dog on the wolf. But the wolf tore the dog's throat out. Then, with an evil howl that sent shivers down the old man's spine, the wolf loped off into the forest.

The Count lay in a puddle of dark red blood. He was still alive but the old man was afraid that the wolf would return. He dared not take the Count to safety until dawn.

Count Vargo recovered from his wounds, but he was a changed man. He began to chew on raw flesh and one night he disappeared. And that's when the howling began. The howls rang through Mercoire Forest and terrified the peasants. Some of them reported seeing a giant wolf. The frightened peasants whispered that the creature was none other than Count Vargo who had become a werewolf – a human that becomes a wolf.

Then the killings began... Men and women were found torn apart. This was no ordinary wolf. Time after time, hunters fired at the beast. And time after time the bullets seemed to strike the wolf only for the beast to escape – unharmed! Perhaps the curse had come true and the Count was the enemy of all other creatures!

Soldiers and hunters searched for the wolf. No one could find it. Even the bravest bloodhounds yelped and cringed in terror when they picked up the beast's scent. All that winter and the following spring, the killings continued, until no one dared to leave their homes. At last, the king sent his huntsman, Antoine de Beauterne, to kill the wolf. Patiently, the huntsman mapped the area, searching for the beast's lair. Then, he led a band of men and dogs to the dark ravine where he thought the wolf lived.

There was a horrible silence. No bird dared to sing. But something was watching from the bushes. Something big and cruel and angry. Then, all at once, the wolf charged. Antoine fired his gun. All the men fired. Their bullets struck the beast again and again, but it didn't fall until its evil heart had bled dry.

At last the wolf was dead, and as for Count Vargo … he was never seen again. But you can be sure he died unhappily ever after!

So what's the boring old truth?

In 1765 a huge wolf killed more than 100 victims, and it was said to be Count Vargo. A second beast was shot in 1767. But scientists don't believe in werewolves and many experts think the creatures were wolf-dog cross-breeds. Hmm – maybe it's time we focused on the facts scientists agree with…

Angry animals fact file

NAME OF CREATURE: Wolf

TYPE OF ANIMAL: Mammal

DIET: Carnivore. Wolves hunt small mammals on their own and band together to kill big animals such as elk.

NUMBER OF PEOPLE KILLED: Wolves sometimes kill people (mostly in India).

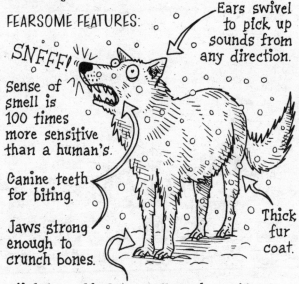

WHERE THEY LIVE: North America (mainly in Canada and Alaska), Russia, Eastern Europe and parts of Asia and India.

SIZE: Male wolves grow to 2 metres long and 85 cm high.

FEARSOME FEATURES:

Ears swivel to pick up sounds from any direction.

SNFFF!

Sense of smell is 100 times more sensitive than a human's.

Canine teeth for biting.

Jaws strong enough to crunch bones.

Thick fur coat.

Slightly webbed toes allow the wolf to run on snow without sinking too much.

Ruthless relatives

Wolves belong to a group of animals called canids, which includes red wolves, coyotes, foxes and dogs. From this group, only wolves and dogs kill humans (see page 115 for the deadly doggie details). But in the USA coyotes are said to give cats nervous breakdowns by staring at them through windows and breathing on the glass (no, honestly, I didn't make that up!).

Canids often live in family groups, and a wolf family is called a pack. So how would you get on in a wolf pack? And could it be any worse than life in your own pack, er, family?

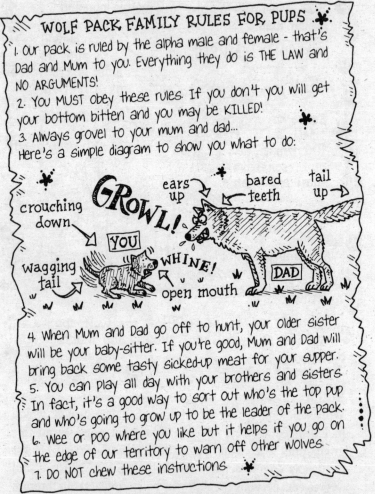

WOLF PACK FAMILY RULES FOR PUPS

1. Our pack is ruled by the alpha male and female - that's Dad and Mum to you. Everything they do is THE LAW and NO ARGUMENTS!

2. You MUST obey these rules. If you don't you will get your bottom bitten and you may be KILLED!

3. Always grovel to your mum and dad...
Here's a simple diagram to show you what to do:

crouching down

ears up

GROWL!

bared teeth

tail up

YOU

wagging tail

WHINE!

open mouth

DAD

4. When Mum and Dad go off to hunt, your older sister will be your baby-sitter. If you're good, Mum and Dad will bring back some tasty sicked-up meat for your supper.

5. You can play all day with your brothers and sisters. In fact, it's a good way to sort out who's the top pup and who's going to grow up to be the leader of the pack.

6. Wee or poo where you like but it helps if you go on the edge of our territory to warn off other wolves.

7. DO NOT chew these instructions.

So much for wolf pups, but what's it like being an adult? Let's take a look at this wolf newspaper...

The Daily Wolf

IN TODAY'S NEWS:
▶ Win a wolf whistle
▶ Wolf spotted in sheep's clothing
▶ Little Red Riding Hood had it coming – a wolf speaks out

WOLF & WOLF

ESTATE AGENTS

We'll keep the wolf from your door!
Looking for a territory to hunt in?
LOVELY BIG TERRITORY IN CANADA
500 square km – and lots of elk to munch! Just the right size for your growing pack!
Also included – deluxe wolf meeting place
• Lots of half-chewed animal bones for pups to play with
• Den for the pups to be born in (OK, it's a hole in the ground but it's a palace for us wolves!)

Just published...
THE WOLF HAPPY HUNTING GUIDE
Find out how to choose the weakest elk in the herd, pull it down and rip it to pieces – it's all down to team-work!

YOU ARE THE WEAKEST ELK... GOODBYE!

"This book really gave me something to get my teeth into. And there weren't too many howling mistakes."
AN Other-Wolf

Just released... THE WOLF PACK'S GREATEST HITS
Listen to one of the greatest packs of our time howling out their most famous songs ... including their chart-topping classic the haunting and heart-warming
"HOWWWWWWWWL – GET OUT OF OUR TERRITORY YOU OTHER WOLVES OR WE'LL RIP YOU TO BITS!"
"Strangely moving – in fact I'm moving to safety right now!" A wolf music critic

If you ask me, wolves sound rather dangerous – and anyone who wants to howl at wolves has the brains of a jellyfish...

Will D Beest in ... Wolf warning

Will and Mickey are in Canada finding out about the world of wolves...

As a top TV naturalist I'm used to danger...

Will he ever learn?

If I howl at wolves, they'll howl back.

Here comes trouble...

HOWOOL! HOWL!

Trouble is, the wolves think I'm another wolf — they may attack.

Now he tells me...

A wolf can scent me 2.5 km away so I'm masking my scent by rolling in rotten fish. Wolves do this to confuse elk.

This plan stinks!

GRRR!

YIKES — I forgot about the grizzlies!

I must say, wolves sound cruel to everyone including other wolves. And if they're as cruel as they're cracked up to be they're a DEAD cert for the Cruellest Creature award. But are they? Well, one thing's certain – humans have killed millions of wolves. Hundreds of years ago, wolves were found all over North America, Europe and most of Asia. But humans have wiped them out in many countries.

- The last wolf in Britain was shot in 1743.
- Nearly every wolf in the USA was killed by the 1920s.
- Wolves were wiped out in France by 1927.

And yet in all that time humans were welcoming millions of wolves into their homes! No, seriously, readers – it's true!

Bet you never knew!

Many scientists believe that dogs are descended from wolves that people once kept to help with hunting. And wolves and dogs still have a lot in common. Both animals show their feelings by making the same sounds and adopting the same positions.

- *They bark to sound a warning, wag their tails when friendly and growl when they're cross.*

WOOF! DANGER!

WAG! HELLO!

GRRR! DINNER!

- *Does your dog whine and try to lick you when it wants feeding? Wolf pups do this to get their parents to feed them. If you sicked-up some meat your dog might even want to lick it up.*

113

- *If your dog whines and grovels when you're cross with it, it probably thinks you're its pack leader.*
- *Does your dog enjoy sniffing lampposts and peeing on them or leaving you-know-whats in certain places? That's how wolves mark their territory, and your dog probably thinks you own the street.*

For 10,000 years humans have bred dogs to look different from wolves. And we've developed a very close friendship with dogs ... *most* of the time.

Barking mad quiz

Which of these three so-called dog facts are true and which one is a shaggy dog story?

1 In 2003 a Japanese company invented a machine that translates dog sounds into human speech.

2 A Brazilian doctor trained his pet dog to help with surgical operations.

3 A dog was once a king in Norway.

Answer:

1 TRUE – Japanese toy maker Takara has created a device called Bowlingual that picks up the sounds made by dogs, works out the sound patterns and turns them into a message. They've made a similar device for cats.

114

2 FALSE – Would you want a doggie doctor or a Fido physician? I hope not – dogs can be DANGEROUS!!!

3 TRUE – According to legend, King Eystein conquered his enemies and made them choose his dog as their ruler. I bet the dog made everyone else bow-wow to him.

Fido the Fearsome

Most dogs have been bred and trained *not* to attack humans, but some of them can be a menace…

1 Parts of the USA and Europe have been terrorized by wild dogs (mostly unwanted pets). These prowling packs include all types of dogs but they're usually led by big dogs such as Alsatians.

2 In the USA, every year about 18 people are killed by dogs and about 300,000 need hospital treatment. In fact, deadly dogs kill and injure more people than sharks, snakes, bears and mountain lions put together!

3 In 2001, wild dogs known as dingos killed a boy on Fraser Island, Australia.

4 Some breeds, such as pit-bull terriers, have been bred to fight other dogs. In most countries dog fights are against the law but in 2002 thieves in California tried to steal a litter of pit-bull puppies to train them to fight. Unfortunately they stole chihuahua puppies by mistake…

I guess those thieves were dogged by misfortune and now they're in the doghouse.

So where does all this leave our Cruellest Creature Competition? Is the treasured trophy going to the dogs – or are we barking up the wrong tree? Well, don't go away – I'VE JUST HEARD WE'VE GOT A RESULT!

At last – the news you've all been waiting for…
Welcome to the Anytown Zoo! We're here to announce the winner of the Horrible Science Cruellest Creature Competition. All the animals in this book are here except for the great white shark (no one's been brave enough to invite him).

And here to make the announcement is Will D Beest…

THE WORLD'S CRUELLEST CREATURE?

And here to receive the award is Honest Bob.

Oh dear, there are scenes of uproar in the hall. Will's looking upset, the animals are angry and Bob's run off with the trophy. We asked Will why he's so unhappy at the result…

I think Will's got a point. So I asked the judges to explain their decision…

Is that really true? Let's see if the judges are right. Do humans really kill more dangerous animals than they kill us? Well, the figures are a bit sketchy – but here's a fascinating figure about sharks...

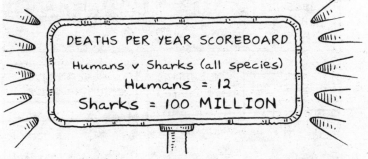

DEATHS PER YEAR SCOREBOARD

Humans v Sharks (all species)

Humans = 12

Sharks = 100 MILLION

And look at all the crocodiles and buffaloes and bears and tigers and lions and wolves that humans have killed over the years. OK, we'd better agree with the judges on numbers. But what about us being able to wipe out other animals. Surely that's a bit over the top?

Er, no it's not...

Remember all that stuff about food webs and habitats? (Take a look back to page 11 if you don't.) Food webs mean that animals depend on each other for food. But when humans take over a habitat the food web unravels faster than your granny's knitted jumper. And since the big carnivores at the top of the food chains need lots of herbivores to hunt, they're in great danger of going hungry. Let's visit Wolf Forest in North America...

OK, so I made up Wolf Forest – but many of the animals in this book are going hungry as humans take over their habitats. We've seen it with elephants and bears and lions and tigers. And when the wild animals eat the humans' livestock or crops the humans turn nasty and the animals are in danger…

Let's see what this means for some of the animals in this book. I've invented a machine called an Extinct-o-meter. All you do is press the button for each animal and find out how many are left. If the animal's in danger of becoming extinct (dying out) a siren sounds…

ANIMALS LEFT IN THE WILD

Indian elephants - fewer than 40,000 ○

Lions - fewer than 20,000 ○

Tigers - fewer than 1,000 ○

Pandas - fewer than 1,000 ○

Neeeeeeeeegh!

Is this really necessary?

Hmm – it really does look as if humans could wipe out some species of animals in this book. It's a good thing no one's shooting animals for money and selling off their body bits… Oh dear, look what I've just found!

Honest Bob's Animal Body Bits shop

All our products are guaranteed illegal, so if you see any cops you don't know me - right?*

Brighten up your home and scare the cat with a traditional **tiger-skin rug**. Warning - keep clear of the sharp teeth!

ORIENTAL MEDICINES

Bear bile slurp - lovely **bear's gall bladder** (that's the bit that stores digestive juices from the liver). It's good for your guts and your heart.

 Delicious **tiger-bone tonic wine**. It's good for your joints and it boosts your brainpower!

Tiger skull. Sleep on it and you won't have nightmares (traditional Chinese belief).

 Lovely **leopard-skin coat**. You'll feel a million dollars in this luxury coat - so that's what I'll charge you!

Genuine wild **crocodile-skin shoes** and matching handbags. Ideal for the snappy dresser!

*DON'T worry, readers, Bob's a con-artist - so he's not selling real animal body bits!

Do you like elephants? You'll love this tasty **elephant meat**. Yes, you can tuck into jumbo-sized steaks.

Trendy ivory jewellery. Made from real **elephant tusks**.

Nasty notes

1 In 2005 experts claimed that poachers in India were killing one tiger every day.

2 Tiger bones do have some painkilling powers – but then so do other animal bones. Bear gall bladders also have medical uses, but man-made substances work just as well.

3 Some people like to eat wild animal meat including the flesh of monkeys and chimps. Can't understand it myself – I mean who'd want to munch a monkey?

HMMMM! MONKEY AND CHIMPS – I MEAN, CHIPS!

DON'T EVEN JOKE ABOUT IT!

Time to sum up. It looks like the judges are right. Some humans are a menace to the animals in this book – but does that make us cruel creatures? Surely we humans have a kinder, gentler side?

I've got a feeling we might find out in the next chapter. Let's hope so – it's the last one!

EPILOGUE: CARING FOR CREATURES

The first Cruellest Creature Competition was held over 500 years ago. In 1459 Count Cosimo de Medici of Florence wanted to find out which animal was fiercest.

But things didn't turn out that way...

The animals were well-fed and, like any well-fed animals, they weren't too keen to fight and risk injury. In fact the cruellest creatures proved to be the humans who set up the terrible test.

Our Horrible Science Cruellest Creature Competition was won by humans, but that doesn't mean we're all cruel. After all, some people really care about animals…

Remember Charles Waterton? Or Subedar Ali trying to save the tiger that attacked him? And *you're* not cruel to animals, are you? Right now many people are trying to save wild animals. Here's an inspiring story that sums up the best and worst about people…

NOW YOU'RE TALKING!

The bumped-off bison

Two hundred years ago the North American plains were thick with bison. You could travel for days and see them all around you. Scientists think they were the biggest herds of wild animals ever. Within 100 years nearly all the bison were dead. Many had been shot by hunters … for FUN!

WHERE ARE YOU, MUM?

BEFORE

MUM?

AFTER

In Europe all the bison had been slaughtered long ago ... except for one herd in the forest of Bialowieza in Poland. In 1914 a battle was fought in the forest and nearly all the bison were killed.

But that's not the end of the story...

In the USA and Europe some bison survived in zoos. Slowly they bred and today bison have returned to the North American plains and the forest of Bialowieza.

This last bit is terribly important. All over the world scientists are studying wild animals in their habitats and trying to find ways to protect them...

• Most countries have already banned the hunting of the animals in this book.

• An international agreement called CITES (Convention on International Trade in Endangered Species) attempts to stamp out the trade in rare animal body bits.

• Zoos are trying to breed rare wild animals in safety. Even if they die out in the wild, some will survive in captivity.

• Some experts think that hunting is a good way to protect habitats – just so long as it's strictly controlled. Many experts are against all hunting.

• More and more tourists visit wild places and some experts hope that the money tourists spend can be used to protect habitats and save their wild animals.

So humans aren't all bad. Some of us might be cruel creatures, but many more of us are caring creatures. And let's hope we're clever enough to choose the best way forward. Happy Horrible Science everyone!

Clever creatures? You're joking!

HORRIBLE SCIENCE

Science with the squishy bits left in!

Ugly Bugs
Blood, Bones and Body Bits
Nasty Nature
Chemical Chaos
Fatal Forces
Sounds Dreadful
Evolve or Die
Vicious Veg
Disgusting Digestion
Bulging Brains
Frightening Light
Shocking Electricity
Deadly Diseases
Microscopic Monsters
Killer Energy
The Body Owner's Handbook
The Terrible Truth About Time
Space, Stars and Slimy Aliens
Painful Poison
The Fearsome Fight For Flight

Specials
Suffering Scientists
Explosive Experiments
The Awfully Big Quiz Book
Really Rotten Experiments

Two horrible books in one
Ugly Bugs and Nasty Nature
Blood, Bones and Body Bits and Chemical Chaos
Frightening Light and Sounds Dreadful
Bulging Brains and Disgusting Digestion
Microscopic Monsters and Deadly Diseases